# The
# ENCOUNTER
## Based Church

## Will Riddle

3rd Edition

Printed in the United States of America

Second Edition: September 2020, & Margins

Third Edition: November 2021

ISBN 978-0-9997895-7-5

# Contents

# Why This Book?

## How I Got Here

I've been a key part of three church plants. In fact, I've spent my most of my adult life as a leader in church plants. The first was in Boston. I was a young leader and teacher for college students in the church. We were part of a Spirit-filled movement that practiced discipleship and believed in the five-fold ministry. It was challenging but fun. We did a lot of things well, but sadly, integrity issues brought the church to an end.

After that experience, my friends and I were ready to try our own thing. We wanted to be in an area that was easier to reach than Boston but not "over-churched" like Dallas where my friends were. So we moved to Cincinnati to start a new church based on the kind of hard core, committed Christianity we believed in. We imagined we could reenact something like *The Cross and The Switchblade* featuring the legendary David Wilkerson. We would pastor people to freedom and bring them the full gospel of salvation, healing, and deliverance.

We started out working with addicts, and soon gathered a respectable-sized group of hungry people. After getting over the initial hurdles and going through some conflicts, I finally got the idea that maybe I should seek special training to learn how to plant a church! Notwithstanding the fact that this was our second plant, and I had graduated from seminary while in Boston, I had had no real training on church planting.

Now if you're a seasoned church leader, I know you're probably thinking, "How crazy could you be to plant a church with no specialized training?" But the kind of hard-core Christianity we were a part of actually blocked out the idea of thinking you might need that kind of training. The basic idea was: if you get the power and presence of God, and are a bold witness for Christ, people will come and you'll make true disciples. It wasn't until I was well along the road to my own church that I started to believe I must be missing something!

*"When the student is ready, the teacher will appear."*

As the saying goes, "When the student is ready, the teacher will appear." God only shows you what you're ready to learn, and I was finally ready to learn about planting a church. It was right at this point that I was introduced to a man who seemed to plant churches as a hobby. He had planted churches in multiple states and talked about it like it was the most natural thing in the world. He made it sound so easy that I was stunned. I asked him what his secret was. That's when he told me about the church planting seminars and coaching he used.

I booked the first trip to a seminar as soon as I could. As the leader talked, all kinds of lights were going on. I saw all of the mistakes I had made as a young church planter. As the saying goes, "if you want to learn Greek, go to seminary, but if you want to learn how to be a pastor, go to *seminars*." I saw that we had done almost everything wrong from the perspective of planting a successful church – although everything we did was a logical consequence of our hard-core Spirit-filled values. As my team and I discussed what it would take to plant a successful church, it became clear that that was not what they felt called to do. We closed our church, shifted gears, and began to do other kinds of ministry.

It was a bit sad for me. I've always harbored the dream of being part of a people who are totally committed to Jesus, reaching and transforming their city in a radical way. A few years later, though, I was given the divine invitation to be a part of another church plant. In this church plant, we did everything exactly according to the same principles I had learned at the seminar. The result was that this church opened its doors at 500 attendees and went up from there. Of course, there were other factors involved as well, but the story of my three church plants is a living experience of the difference between planting a church the way my hard-core background pushed me to do, and the way that seasoned church planters know will work.

## GOALS OF THIS BOOK

That's why I'm writing this book. I've since learned that I'm not alone in this journey at all. A great number of really amazing leaders are struggling to start or to grow their churches on the basic theory that if you just bring power or truth, you'll grow. They're hitting the same walls I hit. Yet if you get advice from the church growth movement, it feels like you're watering down the gospel to draw a big crowd. I'm here to tell you that there is another way. You can have more of God and grow your church at the same time. This is the *Encounter-Based Church*.

> *You can have more of God and grow your church at the same time.*

An *encounter-based* church is one where people are attracted to come, and can then expect to have a dynamic and powerful encounter with Jesus. This book is about how to design an entire church system based on fostering these encounters in healthy ways. It is not a theory book discussing things like the significance of missionality or incarnationalism. It's also not a book teaching you how to have a personal encounter with Jesus. That literature already exists. What I believe is missing is a book which helps you build a healthy thriving church with the goal of focusing the community on encountering Jesus again and again.

There are many resources on helping you build and grow churches. I am truly amazed at the advanced level of content available to church leaders today. The problem is knowing which books to read and which theory to follow. It's easy for a pastor to get trapped in reading paralysis. My hope is that after reading this short book, you'll not only have some good tools, but also some better lenses to help you sort through the existing literature.

If you're familiar with church growth literature already, you'll see here many concepts that you are familiar with, but I believe that by putting them into a new frame, focused on encountering God, we will find fresh gems along a pathway to a thriving Spirit-filled community. I have attended churches that I would call encounter-based, but to my knowledge, no one has ever articulated a theory that would lead someone to create such a church. They are created almost by accident, but are often wildly successful when they are. I'm not trying to invent something new, but rather to describe something that is already proven to work.

I will first address things to help you **get over mental hurdles** that have been keeping you from even thinking about how to grow your church. I feel like the dialogue in the church has stagnated between a few pretty well-established camps who rarely even take notice of one another. These camps are a bit like monasteries where we pray, study and talk with other monks, developing our own habits, culture and ideals. I want to take you outside the monastery and add a few years back to your life by helping you to avoid dead ends, through lessons I learned the hard way.

The next purpose of the book is to **give you a worldview of church growth** that can help you choose the right tactics for your particular church. Many church growth approaches explicitly or implicitly promote the idea that one size fits all. Just redesign your church to look like the system, and magic will happen. Yet, not every tactic works the same way in every context, and not every tactic can even be applied in all contexts, especially if you are in a denominational context or a church renovation. You might have inherited your church, which means you also inherited a culture and its institutional memory. These things create context and take time to change.

It's easy to look at your church or ministry and see what's not working, and then assume you need to make some really big changes. But ironically, small changes can produce big results while big changes often produce chaos and failure. This is because of the iceberg effect: whenever you make a small change, you quickly come across things which are hindering larger changes. As you work to remove the tip of the iceberg, do not be discouraged because they represent something much larger below. I have found that if I am wise in partnering with the Lord, in moving one seemingly small icon, sometimes God moves the entire iceberg and allows me to make much larger changes!

Secondly, large changes are difficult to execute well. People get confused and lose buy-in. When you make a large change, you have very little idea of knowing what is or isn't working. Because many things are changing at once, it is difficult to evaluate any one component. I'll wager to say that even if you're looking to make big changes in your church, the simple answer is the one you need most.

Another reason why the worldview is more important than the tactics is that the organism of the church operates fundamentally differently at different orders of magnitude or scale. A church of 100 and a church of 10,000 have very little in common except that they both have a person they call "Pastor." My belief here is that when you catch the worldview of the encounter-based church, that you as a leader will be able to apply it in the way that is right for where you are.

From this orientation, my goal is to **give you some key strategies and tactics** that you should be able to apply directly or adapt to your own context. I also want to help you **deal with a few pitfalls** which are common to church leaders. While I'm not pretending to be a church growth guru, you and I probably have more in common than you do with the church growth experts or mega-church pastors that most of us look to for guidance—because the majority of us are planters or leaders in small to medium-sized contexts with significantly smaller resources and name recognition. I've now spent more than twenty years in this playing field, and my role as a parachurch ministry executive in a large national organization has given me many lessons which I believe also apply in the church as well.

Ministers are incredibly busy, and often quite widely read. This is book is short so that it can be practical and applicable. The level of complexity of some of the church growth resources available can literally boggle the mind. I don't want you to become a professional student. Let's find things you can do now. Let's find some simple, practical suggestions you can easily apply to your own context and see the growth you're looking for.

# Embracing Growth

## FOUR POLES

My observation is that there are four basic ways that people think about church growth—that their church will grow primarily through Truth being preached, through the power of the Holy Spirit, through Community, or through Systems. If you were to put these on a diagram, it might look like this:

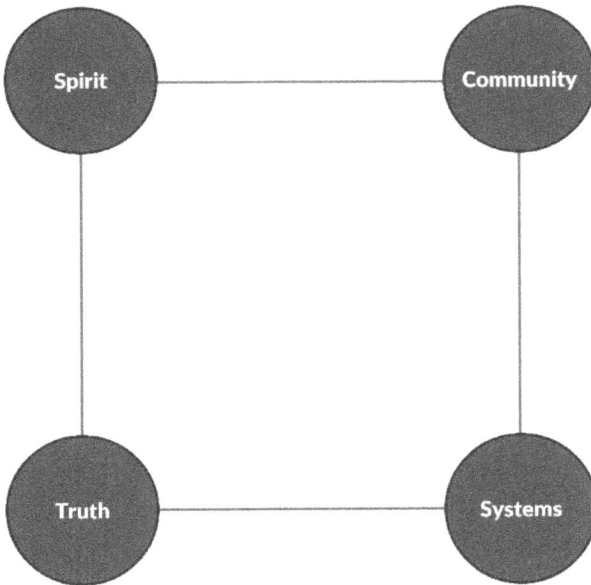

In my experience, for the most part, leaders will tend to place all of their emphasis or one or two factors, almost to the exclusion of the others. How about you? If you were to place a pin in the square above, representing how much you lean on each of these, where you would you place it? If you're not sure, think about it as I describe them further.

**Truth.** For those with a Truth mindset, the idea is that you will grow your church through proclaiming the truth better and more boldly than others. Truth is what will bring people to salvation. Truth will also fix people's problems. If you preach the Word of God plainly and build your church on teaching the Bible, growth will happen as a logical result because people will hear the gospel and abandon their sins.

An exclusively Truth oriented mindset leads pastors to spend most of their energy mining the Word and creating sermons to properly instruct their congregation. A Truth focus also tends to accompany a belief that real evangelism is almost always one-to-one cold-reach witnessing—so there's a push that the church needs to do a lot more of that. While once the dominant view of evangelism in American Christianity, it is probably only explicitly held by a small segment of the church now. But many of us nevertheless subconsciously hold some aspects of this viewpoint.

**Holy Spirit.** Next, there are those with a Holy Spirit mindset. The idea here is that if you earnestly seek the Lord, the power of God will draw people into church supernaturally. When they arrive, they will then be converted by the power of the Holy Spirit—especially healing, miracles and prophecy. In this mindset, the idea is that we really need only focus vertically on the First Commandment—loving God with everything we have—because everything else will logically follow.

This is the predominant viewpoint in many Charismatic churches. In fact, it is so dominant that evangelism is rarely mentioned as its own topic, and when we do mention it, we focus on the coolest stories that come from going out in public to do healings and prophetic ministry. The view of evangelism is still personal witnessing but enhanced with the power of the Holy Spirit.

While I definitely agree that if you are moving in the same level of power as Jesus you will attract a lot of people, that doesn't necessarily translate into church growth. First of all, while I've been privileged to be friends with a few very anointed people, none of them are currently doing the miracles of Jesus on a regular basis. But for those who are closest to walking in high levels of power actually have traveling ministries or schools, rather than churches. This is partly because that's what the body needs, but also partly because growing a church takes grace and insight specific to the task. Jesus' ministry was not limited to personal witnessing or miracles. He did many kinds of ministry and events, and the more I have looked at it, the more I believe there was a strategy behind it. So miracles are an essential aspect of God's Kingdom, but they are not the only key to building a vibrant church that is reaching people.

**Community.** If having the Holy Spirit is about the First Commandment and being connected vertically to God, then having Community is about the Second Commandment and being connected horizontally to each other. Those with this mindset recognize that deep and meaningful relationships are something everyone needs and many people crave.

The operating idea behind the Community mindset of growth is that the New Testament church was primarily a close-knit community where everyone was fully known and fully engaged, so that we can and should be as well. The implication is that anything less than this kind of community is actually less than Biblical. Moreover, since in our atomized modern world most people lack this kind of community, if we create it, the church will organically grow.

In my experience most people with the Community mindset are either trying to replicate an awesome community they experienced before, or reacting against the experience they had in a large church which felt anonymous and media-driven. The first challenge is that awesome community is very difficult to form, because it involves hidden factors that are hard to replicate. It is often catalyzed by a highly relational person or people in exactly the right setting

The second challenge is that great community is usually also very insular. Once people start to feel comfortable and like each other, the community becomes more and more focused inward. It's great for everyone who is knit in, but not for those who are not. And it's a closed system which by nature stays small. It's a community and it's authentic, but it will remain small.

**Systems.** In the church growth movement, there has been a recognition that the nuts and bolts of the church—its Systems—are crucial to bringing in the lost. A Systems mindset scrutinizes every aspect of church life from the Sunday message, to the worship, to the way things look and feel. The church is transformed from services primarily focused on believers, to those focused on outsiders.

When I first heard about Systems, it actually bent my mind quite a bit because I had only been exposed to the other lines of thinking. I was actually shocked at the idea that evangelism could be done through the church service itself—as opposed to street outreach or prophetic evangelism. The idea is that effective evangelism occurs as the church meeting is designed to facilitate it. If you're doing it right, the church itself becomes the most powerful way to meet Jesus. Personal outreach is always important, but it's a lot more effective with the church itself in the middle. A great church will act like a magnet, which draws people in.

The catch to the Systems mindset of growth is that it can work so well that it drifts from Truth, Community, and the Holy Spirit to just a good marketing engine. It can lead us down a formula driven path, which takes the life out of church, becoming an end unto itself. Attendance numbers can become a proxy for changed lives and all the other things God is doing in the church. In addition, if we have succeeded in making our church a place that people want to come, the size of the front door can mask the size of the back door. We want systems which don't just attract but build and maintain a vibrant body of believers experiencing authentic transformation.

My contention is that all four of these poles are needed in order for a church to be really healthy and growing. If only one

*If only one is emphasized, you get something that either doesn't reach, doesn't touch, or doesn't matter.*

is emphasized, you get something that either doesn't reach, doesn't touch, or doesn't matter. We need a new theory that accounts for all of these factors, but gives us a new North Star which can help stay focused. This is the *encounter-based* church. When you combine Truth, the Holy Spirit, Community, and effective Systems, you create an environment for *encounter* – a place where people who have not yet met Jesus will encounter Him in a dynamic and living way, and where those who already know him can continually be refreshed and drawn down a path of growth.

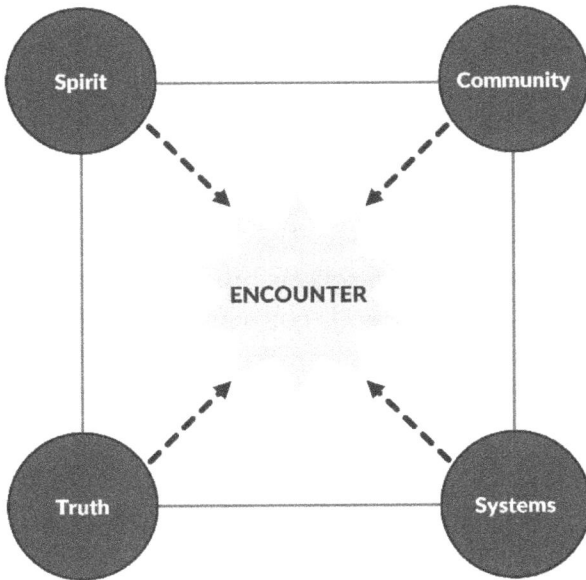

I believe the reason why we tend to be so polar in our attempts to create church is that each of these four avenues to growth—Truth, Spirit, Community, and Systems—exist as part of a larger worldview of what it means to be a Christian. Advocates of each don't believe in them in isolation but as extensions of other things in Christianity. This makes it hard to adjust from one pole to another, or to find resources which address more than one. To go on this journey with me, you'll have to be willing to come outside of the monastery you may have unknowingly been living in.

My friends and I were in the radical Christianity monastery. We spent time watching videos of hard-core revivalists, reading the works of old evangelists and church history. These radical stories told us that if we would just be more radical we would get better results. But the thing about stories is that we tell them not because they are normal, but precisely because they are not normal. Furthermore, we emphasize those parts of the stories that reinforce what we already want to hear. Regardless of exactly which pole you are starting from, this phenomenon creates an echo chamber that you almost have to be shocked out of to escape.

### INSIGHT FROM THE TABERNACLE

The Lord led an entire people out of Egypt once. Many of them weren't sure if they wanted to know Him, and some weren't even sure if they even wanted out of Egypt! Yet God had a plan to bring them into relationship with Him. This plan is modeled in the Tabernacle. The Tabernacle ingeniously created several rings of fellowship where were based on the level of consecration and connection of the people there. Because we no longer live in Old Covenant, making offerings, we often overlook the wisdom of God that is built into this design, but a closer look shows what I believe are very important principles for building a church in the contemporary era. I'm not going to give a full teaching on the Tabernacle, but I want to draw some principles out that I believe are relevant to leading a church.

In the center of the Tabernacle was the Holy of Holies where the Ark of God's Presence resided. *At the center of everything we do must be the presence of God.* If the presence of God is not at the core of what we do the other portions are meaningless. It is impossible to come into the presence of God and not be changed. Secondly, those who entered the Holy of

Holies were specially consecrated for this purpose, and did not live there, but only came on occasion, as it was a place of dramatic encounter—there was a veil which separated the Holy of Holies from the rest of the Tent of Meeting.

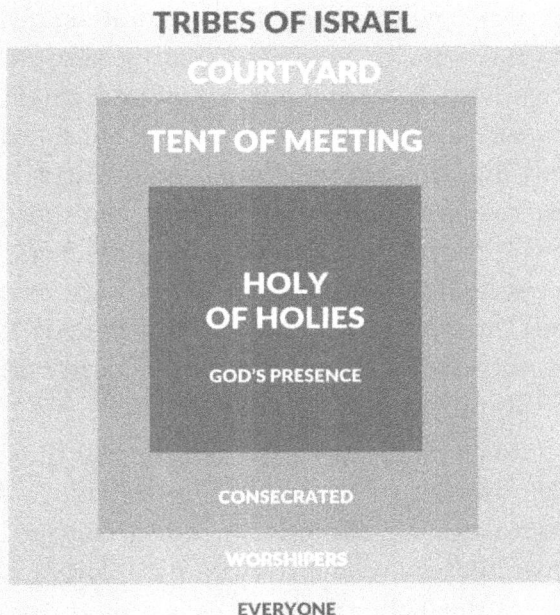

TRIBES OF ISRAEL
COURTYARD
TENT OF MEETING
HOLY
OF HOLIES
GOD'S PRESENCE
CONSECRATED
WORSHIPERS
EVERYONE

In the Tent of Meeting, were a few key things, including the lampstand, which is the illumination of the Holy Spirit, the altar of incense, which represents prayer, and table of showbread, which represents communion and fellowship. The Tent of Meeting is a place of fellowship for the consecrated. Those who have set themselves apart for prayer and fellowship are able to fellowship in the light of the Holy Spirit.

The Tent was placed into a courtyard. This Courtyard (usually referred to as the Outer Court) contained an altar for sacrifice and then a washbasin for cleansing. These two consecrating steps had to be accomplished before anyone could enter the Tent itself. Jesus Himself is our sacrifice and his blood cleanses us from sin. When we preach His crucifixion and invite people to be baptized, we are ministering the reality of the Courtyard. Anyone who comes in by the gate of Jesus and is ready to put their sins on the altar and be cleansed can fellowship in the outer court.

My observation is that most churches are either set up like a Tent of Meeting *or* like a Courtyard. We either make them places where those who are highly consecrated and hungry can come and fellowship, or we make them a place where those who need cleansing from sin can repent and be cleaned. This is not necessarily something we do intentionally, it's just a natural extension of our individual vision and background. Some of us, recognizing and hungering for the presence of God, build our church like the Tent, while others, desiring to reach lost people, build our church like the Courtyard. What I believe the Tabernacle teaches us, however, is that to truly fulfill God's purposes we must have both expressions, and the presence of God must be at the center.

Rather that separate off the community of the consecrated from the community of those finding salvation – as we are highly prone to do, we should figure out how to maintain a community of the consecrated within the larger community, just as we see in the Tabernacle. This is how those who are on the outside will discover and come to desire the deeper fellowship which is only available to those who are consecrated.

Remember the Tent was only illuminated by the light of the Spirit, but the Courtyard had natural light. In other words, there was a completely different atmosphere. The thought process of those being led by the Spirit and those who are just discovering the Lord from the outside world is completely different, and so their interests and needs are different as well. If you want to build a church that has both elements, you have to take this into account. By default, a church that is only focused on salvation tends to bore or starve the consecrated, and a church focused on deep things seems irrelevant to those who have never encountered Him before.

Keep in mind also that the Tent was small, but the

Courtyard was large. If you set up your church like a Tent of Meeting, expect it to be small. At any place and any time there is only a small number of people ready to devoted to a lifestyle of living in the presence. Conversely, if you set up your church like the Courtyard, the church can be much larger, but large numbers can create the illusion of success. If people are not ultimately encountering the presence of God, not much is really happening.

Finally, note that the Tribes of Israel all encamped around the Tabernacle. This meant that every living member of Israel, whether they had any personal relationship with God or interest in God was only steps away from being reconciled with Him through the Tabernacle. By setting up a "Tabernacle" in our community, we can have an impact on the entire culture around us. This is goal of the church – to change the world around us, bringing God's presence and His ways from heaven to the earth.

It should be noted that many many more people were camped outside the Tabernacle than inside. Some church leaders have discovered that if they speak generic language to the masses outside they can attract a large following, but I believe this fundamentally confuses the meaning of a church. The Courtyard gives us clarity in that regard: in order to be a church, we must present the Gate, who is Jesus, the altar his sacrifice, and the cleansing from sin through his blood. There is always the need for ministering the truth of Jesus to the culture at large, and when we are outside in the culture we must speak the language of the culture, but we should never confuse that with what happens inside the church itself.

As you are thinking about the church you lead or wish to build, ask yourself: Does the expression I'm creating welcome the lost or the hungry? Do I have expressions which will speak to the needs of both the consecrated and those who need Jesus? Do I have a clear pathway from outside the camp to the Holy Place?

## PERMISSION TO INNOVATE

I was completely oblivious in the early years of my ministry of why anything other than the raw power of the Holy Spirit might be needed to grow a church. A complex set of reasons and relationships had me trapped inside my own personal monastery. I think like many people who have been starved in an environment without at emphasis on the Holy Spirit, that once I discovered Him, I pursued fresh experiences like there was nothing else on the planet. While this passion is certainly commendable, the long view of life has educated me that God is also the wise master builder.

One of the reasons why I was stuck in my thinking was a narrow view of "church." After deep Bible study, I simply thought that if we simply read the Scripture and tried to do what they said, it would work. What I now realize is that every church model created since Martin Luther and John Calvin hashed out the Reformation has claimed to be *the* Biblical model of church and will cite appropriate passages of Scripture to support it. What many experts on ecclesiology have concluded, however, after centuries of wrestling, is that the Bible does not give an exact manual for how to set up a church! It does, however, give principles and tactics both for running a church as well as reaching the lost. This is borne out as you look at how church structure has evolved not just since the Reformation, but even in the last several decades.

The fallacy that had me trapped in this way of thinking was not appreciating context. In seminary, one of the principles that teachers drill into you is that the epistles of the New Testament are "occasional" in nature. This means most of them were written to specific people for specific reasons. In other words, context matters. While the epistles communicate universal truths, in order to understand those universal truths properly, you must do your best to first understand the context in which they were spoken. It's a simple idea, but one that is often overlooked. Context is an important part of interpreting all statements, including those in the Word.

If you just lift a random passage out of the Bible without any context and apply it to all scenarios, there is a reasonable chance that you're applying it wrong. God doesn't say the same exact thing to same to everyone all the time. For the rich young ruler, it was: "Sell everything you have and come follow me." For the man on the mat it was: "Take heart, son, your sins are forgiven." Imagine the disaster if you reversed the words given to these two men! To know which one of these applies best to your life at any given moment, or to a person you are ministering to, you have to look at the context. That's why context is king.

What we need to do is look at our current context and apply the Scripture correctly to it. The context in which we live is modern Western society, which has gone through enormous changes in the last 500 years. As culture and technology have changed, the church has adapted in order to continue to reach the world around us. This is a good thing! Models which work well grow while those that do not work fade away. You judge a good tree by its fruit, and one of the key fruits we want to examine is if it grows. The sign of a healthy tree is growth.

World-famous sociologist Rodney Stark has pointed out that European countries with their government-based churches became secular much more quickly than America with its freedom of religion. Stark further theorizes that this is because of the free market. In Europe, there was no room to innovate and therefore the church became irrelevant, while in America the best and most effective ways to reach the world were discovered through great experimentation.

I recently met a Swedish man at the airport. After we talked for a while, the conversation turned to matters of religion, and I asked him if he went to church. The state-run Lutheran church, which seemed totally disconnected from the concerns of his modern life, was the only context he had to even think about that question, and while he was clearly hungry, the 16th century church model was not going to provide any food. The lack of innovation in church and the disconnection of Swedish society from God were personified by his life.

In the United States, freedom of religion has meant that we are free to explore and pursue God in any variety of formats. One direct result of this freedom is that America was the incubator for the growing global move of the Holy Spirit, first launched from Azusa street in Los Angeles in 1906 . We had freedom to invite and build around Him and this trajectory has continued as we have sought to build churches on a greater understanding of the work of the Holy Spirit, where the power of God was welcomed became centers of revival and transformation. The openness to innovation that exists in the free American system is actually a key factor which made room for God to come and also to build in ways that better facilitated His design.

We must find what God is doing in our generation and the wise blueprints He has given us to build now. The truth is always the same, but the context continually changes. What has worked somewhere else may not work here, and what worked here even 30 years ago, may not work now. This is not because the truth has changed, but because context has changed. A new context requires a different emphasis on different truths. We need new wineskins for the new wine. How do we put together a model which is both firmly Biblical as well as effective in the world of Amazon.com and the smartphone?

## THE CHURCH GROWTH MOVEMENT

I believe part of the answer lies in taking a fresh look at the Church growth movement. One of the founders of the church growth movement, the legendary missiologist Donald McGavran, was descended from a long line of missionary leaders, going back to the days of William Carey in India. He was inspired by the Student Volunteer Movement to dedicate his own life to mission work. As he observed the wildly different success of some movements in India compared to the established mission paradigm, he sought to examine why some succeeding and others weren't. He said:

> Acting on advice given to me by the great missionary statesman, John R. Mott, I had determined to challenge every assumption that I could recognize as underlying the work of my Church in India, not to prove any of them wrong, but to find out, if I could, whether they seemed to be right or wrong as indicated by their results.[1]

This led him to a progressive and methodical study of church growth on the mission field, including 17 years of putting his theories into practice. The eventual result was the ground-breaking book *The Bridges of God* and later his book *How Churches Grow*. These books launched a movement in the United States of examining how to reach our own society by examining what actually worked to bring about real conversions and subsequent discipleship in the church.

While this may not sound radical, it definitely was, and to some people, still is. We tend to think we can discover the truth by naked reading of Scripture without any thought about our own time and biases. But I believe this is where the fruit principle can help us immensely: We're not simply trying to reason up from the Scripture as I was when I started planting churches, but by looking at the fruit, we can know if we are applying the Scripture properly to our context. And that's exactly what McGavran set out to do.

As McGavran and his disciples at Fuller Theological Seminary began to observe the patterns of growth in the global church, one of the common denominators which emerged was an emphasis on the Holy Spirit. Globally speaking, all of the world's largest churches are Spirit-filled in orientation. And in particular, in the 70's and early 80's, the Yoido Full Gospel Church in South Korea led by Dr. David Yonngi Cho was stunning the world with its massive success. People all over the world flocked to copy his method of cell group ministry.

---

[1]From "Donald McGavran: Missionary, Scholar, Ecumenist, Evangelist." In *God, Man and Church Growth*. J. Waskom Pickett, ed. Grand Rapids, MI: Eerdmans.

Shortly after, in Latin America, huge churches sprang up seemingly overnight. But in the United States, no one was able to get an exact copy working, which has led to generations of leaders testing and tweaking the cell group model trying to become the American Dr. Cho. C. Peter Wagner was a key figure in this wave of the Church Growth movement, and so was his guest lecturer, the man who went on to become the founder of the Vineyard movement and author of *Power Evangelism*, John Wimber.

The iconic zenith of the church growth movement was the explosion of Willow Creek church in the Chicago suburbs in the 1980s and 1990s. By applying church growth principles, Bill Hybels was able to build what was then America's largest church. He captured the imagination of pastors around the country. His concept was to be "seeker sensitive." Leaders would adapt the church, and especially the Sunday service to meet unbelievers who were "seeking" God.

This meant taking a look at every aspect of the church to make sure it was "seeker friendly," including the message itself. The meaty preaching common to most American evangelical pulpits was replaced with much softer messages that were more "relevant" to less-churched people. Many were saved through this approach, but some also floated around in a shallow version of Christianity, as the church's own self-evaluation called REVEAL demonstrated in 2008.

In parallel, Rick Warren, a young seminary graduate, was exploring why his neighbors did not want to go to church. The answers he found were: boredom, irrelevance to everyday life, feeling unwelcomed, focusing on money and poor children's programs. As Warren started addressing these issues, the small Southern Baptist church he led started to grow, and over time he became one of the leading pastors in America.

A major idea in his book, *The Purpose Driven Church,* was to grow the church without compromising the truth. He had some excellent insights that I'm going to build on, but as a traditional Southern Baptist, I don't think he had a strong awareness of the presence of God or how to accommodate for it in his approach. When we bring the Holy Spirit into the picture, it opens up another dimension of possibility, that we should actively engage.

A key member of Warren's team in the early days was another successful Southern Baptist evangelist and church planter named Nelson Searcy, who was added to help launch churches around the country. Searcy was trained in computer science and analyzed everything, boiling it down into repeatable processes, and now coaches church planters and leaders around the country to success. The focus is on having good systems that draw people in and build them up.

Over time, the largest and most successful churches in America have developed a high level of skill with production and media, leading to the concept of the *attractional* church. The idea here is that if you make your Sunday service the kind of event that people want to come to – excellent, well-polished with best in class media, you will attract people to come.

In the book, *The Attractional Church* by Steve Hornsby, he uses the analogy of a very memorable visit he had to a Rolls Royce showroom to communicate this concept. He wanted to return to this dealership because the experience was so excellent. The idea is to try and replicate that level of service and excellence as a way of making the church a place that people are attracted to and want to come back to.

In essence, the attractional church concept applies the insights of modern marketing and customer service to the church experience. While at one point in my life I would have outright rejected this idea, now that I've had many different leadership experiences inside and outside of church, I see it as common sense. You would never start any other kind of organization unless you had a plan to attract clients, and then planned to serve them very well when they came. All of the largest churches in America are applying church growth

*The modern church growth movement actually arose from a desire to see what the Holy Spirit was doing and replicate it.*

principles to some degree or another because if you do not apply them, you can't build a large church, just like you can't build a business without marketing and customer service.

At the same time, many of those who understand this have a tendency to treat it as a magic formula. But that's also a fundamental mistake that any business person would recognize. Marketing and customer service are essential to running a business, but ultimately you must have an awesome product. In the case of a church, the "product" is life change through personal encounter with Jesus. If you are not providing that, all of the King's horses and all of the King's men are not going to be able to make it grow.

It should not be a case of either/or. The modern church growth movement actually arose from a desire to see what the Holy Spirit was doing and replicate it. Over time, however, these two streams came apart. Those interested in the working of the Holy Spirit became more and more focused on having more of the Spirit, while those interested in church growth became more and more focused on marketing and systems to identify tweaks to the church that would bring more people. The divorce has led to tiny Charismatic churches where anything goes, and giant megachurches scripted down to the second.

These things should not be. I believe the church growth movement was a Holy Spirit phenomenon from the beginning, and it's time to return to its roots.

## JESUS IS ATTRACTIONAL

Some have convinced themselves that since the message of Jesus is a hard message, anything we do that might attract people is a form of compromise. But look at the meeting that

Jesus held in Capernaum. Huge crowds were following Him and He explains why in John 6:26:

> Very truly I tell you, you are looking for me, not because you saw the signs I performed but because you ate the loaves and had your fill.

They didn't come for the truth or because of Jesus Himself. They didn't even come for the miracles. They came for the food that He and the disciples were serving! Jesus then goes on to tell them that they should be coming to find eternal life.

Jesus was fully aware that an unregenerate person is looking with their five senses, not with a spiritual eye, and so I believe he leveraged this insight to his advantage. After all "no one can see the kingdom of God unless they are born again." (John 3:3). They were only able to see the natural, so He offered them something natural as the gateway to the spiritual. By meeting physical needs, He was able to create openness to address spiritual needs. I think where this can get derailed is when we see the crowds that food can draw, and become a restaurant instead of a church. People may be attracted by a great meal, but they are changed when they encounter the Holy Spirit there.

*An encounter-based church is one where people are attracted to come, and can then expect to have a dynamic and powerful encounter with Jesus.*

An *encounter-based* church is one where people are attracted to come, and can then expect to have a dynamic and powerful encounter with Jesus. Too often we see either one or the other. A leader has either embraced church growth principles or the Holy Spirit almost to the exclusion of the other. Yet they are designed to go together. People who have relied strictly on marketing and systems have missed the fact that nothing in the world is more attractional than Jesus. Those of us who have had a profound personal encounter with Him through the Holy Spirit know that nothing even comes close. As the Psalmist says, He is "more to be desired than gold, and sweeter than honey in the honeycomb." (Ps 19:10).

In other words, the things which may attract someone in the natural cannot compare with the spiritual attractiveness of Jesus. This is one of the reasons why He can say, "If I am lifted up from the earth I will draw all people to Myself" (John 12:32). When we create an environment where people can encounter this Jesus, everything changes. There is no coffee or lights or beautiful entryway that is going to hold a candle to the presence of Jesus. Excellence (or great food) may help bring them in, but without encounter, you'll never keep them in.

On the other hand, by downplaying people's human needs and telling them that if they don't like our shabbiness or our salty truths it's because they are worldly, we're misrepresenting the character of Jesus. Jesus did have salty truths for hardened people like the Pharisees, but for those seeking Him, He served day and night to meet their very human needs. Disabled people walked again, people with diseases were healed and blind eyes were opened. He did this because He cared about them, and He was a caring person. He was the kind of person you'd like to meet. If we are going to build a church that represents Him, we can start by creating a wonderful and inviting place because He is a wonderful and inviting person!

## THE HOLY SPIRIT FOR EVERYONE

When we hold Charismatic services where there is no order, we misrepresent Jesus as being either someone who is weird or is not interested the average person. Jesus proved Himself to be incredibly "normal" and relatable to people of all backgrounds because He loved them so much. We want to hold services that manifest this kind of love. That is what I believe Paul had in mind in 1 Corinthians 14:

> If the whole church comes together and everyone speaks in tongues, and inquirers or unbelievers come in, will they not say

that you are out of your mind?...But if an unbeliever or **an inquirer comes in while everyone is prophesying, they are convicted of sin** and are brought under judgment by all…as the secrets of their hearts are laid bare. So they will fall down and worship God, exclaiming, "God is really among you!"… **Everything must be done so that the church may be built up** (1 Cor. 14:23-26 NIV)

While we have traditionally read this passage as being about the proper use (or non-use) of tongues in a corporate setting, I believe it has a much broader application. It gives us a window into how Paul sees the weekly service. He tells us several important things which I consider the charter of the encounter-based church:

1. We should expect that there will be unbelievers in our services and adjust accordingly.
2. We should be doing things that will edify the Body, not just unbelievers.
3. The power of the Holy Spirit (and specifically prophecy) will reach the lost.

This is an *encounter-based* service. It is a place where we have created an environment that is welcoming to non-believers, but is designed to then bring them into a real encounter with the living God.

These principles give us a very clear road map as to how to hold a service which works for everyone. The Sunday service is designed as the meeting point between any person who is open to meeting Jesus, and Jesus Himself. It is the place where we will encounter Him. So one of our first questions should be: if a person who is open to meeting Jesus comes to my service, will they encounter Him?

On the one hand, Paul explicitly corrects the kind of meetings that some of us who believe in the Holy Spirit like to hold – the kind of service where "anything goes" in the name of the Holy Spirit! Here, Paul uses the example of tongues. If you bring someone who is new to a service where people are all speaking in tongues, they will find it very strange at best.

But that's not the only behavior that falls in this category. People randomly shouting in the middle of the service, or running around the building, or randomly lying on the floor are just a few things that come to mind which are done in the name of freedom of the Spirit—which all but ensure that non-believers will not be present. And not only non-believers – these kinds of behaviors done in the name of the Spirit are often a distraction from a true corporate encounter.

One pastor I know, in his younger days, took a friend to a famous Charismatic church where many of these kinds of things were going on. His seeker friend, who was open enough to come to church with him, punched him in the middle of service and said, "You brought me to a cult!" and walked out. What's surprising is not that his friend walked out, but that he ever walked in. Paul gives us the guideline, and we should obey it if we expect our churches to grow: "Let all things be done decently and in order." (1 Cor. 14:40 NKJV)

Fear of disorder is one of the reasons why many pastors are reticent to really pursue the work of the Holy Spirit in their church. It seems that as soon as you press the "Go" button on the Holy Spirit, someone very unbalanced is going to show up and blow up the meeting and "Charismatic Chaos" will ensue, driving all of the non-believers away. This is an unfortunate result of emphasizing the role of the Spirit's leading to such an extent that to curb such behavior is seen as "quenching the Spirit."

We've created a false dichotomy, where either you run a highly scripted service where you are in control of all elements, or you run a completely unscripted service, where anything goes. What Paul is guiding us toward is neither of these. It is a service where we welcome and cultivate an atmosphere that is conducive to everyone encountering Him corporately, not to ostentatious behavior. Welcoming the Holy Spirit is more like a dance – there are steps, but there is also art.

Paul teaches that in order for the Spirit to function and be present in our meetings, it is essential that we govern the operation of the gifts and create a culture of order. When we fail to govern the operation of the Holy Spirit, what we end up with is giving the flesh permission to masquerade as the Spirit and quench it. It's a little bit like allowing a random person to stand up in the middle of an opera and sing because he's enjoying the music. He is having an amazing time, but it ruins the concert for everyone else. An encounter-based service is about creating an environment where we can **all** have a corporate encounter of Jesus. There is honor, and the Presence.

At the same time, Paul giving instructions on how to govern the flow of the Spirit in a meeting should never be confused with him trying to limit the Holy Spirit. He gives instructions precisely because he *wants* the Spirit to operate and touch people. If you weren't supposed to have the Holy Spirit in your meeting, you wouldn't need these kinds of instructions. Even in the context of these serious corrections he gives to the Corinthians, Paul does not tell them to take the Spirit out of the Sunday meeting, but actually to "***earnestly desire the spiritual gifts***" (1 Cor. 14:1 ESV).

Our problem is not too much of the Holy Spirit, it's too little! Paul not only assumes that we'll have the Holy Spirit, he assumes that such a level of prophetic ministry will be in operation that it could lay the secrets of a visiting person's heart bare and lead them to salvation.

I would further suggest that the ministry of healing and miracles would fit this category as well. The service Paul is talking about is a service where ***people will encounter God.*** It is the junction place between the community of heaven and the community of earth. It's the on-ramp to the family of God. I believe this has been the missing element in the American church growth movement. Once you bring the Spirit back in, God begins to do what only He can do.

# So You Want to Plant a Church?

Statistically, the large majority of church plants fail. If it's safe to assume that most church planters are sincere Christians and also hard-working and talented people, then what can we attribute all of these failures to? I believe most church planters do not know fully what they are getting into and are therefore not ready to do all the things it will take to become successful.

I had this experience myself. A few years into a plant, when my leaders and I discovered what it was really going to take to plant a successful church, we talked it through and the team simply realized they were not interested in doing some of those things. They were not their calling. We closed the church and redirected our energies toward other ministry endeavors.

This is why I want to help you think through some of these things at the outset so you can make the decision with your eyes wide open. In fact, since renovating an existing church requires many of the same commitments that launching a new one does, I encourage you to read this chapter regardless of whether you are leading an existing church or contemplating launching a new one.

Many people are drawn to pastoral ministry because they like to teach or preach, or pastor people. Ironically, while these are very important skills for a pastor, they are actually not the primary responsibility of the senior pastor. The Senior Pastor is first and foremost a leader. You are commissioned like Peter to build the church with Jesus (Matt 16:18). This means you need to develop leaders and put them in places where they participate in the growth of the church. You are to put the "Aces in their places."

Left alone, a medium-sized church will naturally organize itself as a kind of community center with the senior leader as the primary employee. You end up talking about and doing a lot of things that don't directly grow the church or the Kingdom. You have to fight against that trend and tendency. Everything you do should be well-connected to growing the church—this is why you are first a leader. You inspire and commission people to focus outwards, to bring people in.

I recently called my friend Tim who pastors a small church to see how he was doing. He told me he was very busy, too busy in fact to reach back out to some of the unsaved people the Lord had brough him in contact with. So we walked through his schedule to see where the time was going. As we got into the details I discovered that he had tasks on the list like "cut the grass at the church." The pressure on him to be the primary employee of a community center, was crowding out the work God had called him to.

If this is happening to you, don't feel bad, this is the same thing that happened to the twelve apostles in Acts 6. They were getting bogged down in practical concerns and pulled away from God's assignment to feed the sheep the spiritual bread they needed. This is why they commissioned and anointed the deacons they realized that, "It is not right that we should give up preaching the word of God to serve tables." (Acts 6:2). These deacons were empowered to serve and then went on to do their own great exploits – true ministry multiplication. Fortunately for my friend, he made adjustments and began to put his energy in the right places and see fruit from it. Have you commissioned people to serve with you, or are you still "cutting the grass"?

The nuts and bolts of launching a church have been highly refined by groups like the Association of Related Churches (ARC) and Nelson Searcy's coaching network. I'm going to be touching lightly on something they have turned into a science. If you are considering launching a church, I highly encourage you to connect with a church planting group that can support your launch. Be aware, however, that groups that launch churches normally have a strong understanding of systems and church growth, but not an equally strong emphasis on the presence of God. You will have to bring that in order to create encounters in your church. This book is not designed to tell you every last thing you need to know about starting a church, but to help you navigate the landscape and bring a flavor I believe is missing elsewhere.

## WHAT IS A CHURCH?

Starting a church is a very idealistic endeavor. For most of us it's our opportunity to fulfill a dream of how Christianity can or should be. We think through things from the bottom-up with specific values and goals in mind. For our team in Cincinnati, that was informed both by our passion for supernatural ministry and by our desire to have servant leadership after the top-down experiences we'd all had.

We spent a great deal of time hashing out a statement of faith, a statement of values, and other documents. While these things definitely had value, this kind of focus fundamentally misunderstands what a church is, and how to grow one. I'm not going to give a deep theological definition of the ἐκκλησία. While that often makes for an interesting sermon, this is a practical book so will give you a practical definition: *A church is a voluntary gathering of people who encounter Jesus and reach the world together.*

Whenever you are missing one of these elements, the church will falter. First, the church is *voluntary*. Jesus started the church with the beautiful invitation to His disciples to "Come follow Me" (Matt 4:9). Understanding the invitational nature of what you are doing is extremely important. People are making a choice whether or not they want to follow you, and follow Jesus with you, or not. In order for this to happen, we must extend the invitation for them to do so, and usually we must do so in many different ways and contexts.

This invitation is required to get people in the door, but then the invitation continues at every step of the journey. Just as Jesus continually invited His disciples into deeper and higher levels of discipleship, so do we. And because it is an invitation, if someone does not want to take the next step on the journey, we do not pressure them – we allow them to make their own choice about how close or how far they want to be. Save yourself a lifetime of heartache by inviting but not pressuring. Give people space to have their own journey, but continually point them to the next step they can take when they are ready.

Secondly, the church is a *gathering*. We can have great experiences with God individually – and in fact, our most common and often most powerful experiences of God are individual ones. But assembling together as a corporate body presents unique possibilities. By yourself, you cannot be "the body of Christ," you can only be a one part of the body. Together with others, you can express all of the aspects of who He is, including, perhaps most importantly, His deep desire for relationship.

Understanding that the church is a gathering sheds light on what we are doing as leaders. We put energy into assembling the gathering. "Gather" is an active verb – it is something that you proactively do, and it is a fundamental role of the church leadership to create a space where people want to gather, and then to put energy into bringing people into that gathering. While teaching, preaching, and worship are essential, they will not matter very much if no one is gathered to experience them.

Once we are gathered, our first purpose and focus is *to worship and encounter Jesus*. Without Jesus, church is like a cookie without sugar, or a stew with no meat – no matter how great the other parts are, you can't hide the fact that the main ingredient is missing! When we come together in corporate worship, bringing an offering of prayer, praise and thanksgiving, putting Him first, we bring a little piece of heaven down to earth both in the lives of individuals present, and the corporate experience itself.

All of our preaching and teaching must lead us back to

Him as well. We're not trying to change lives with new doctrine or great stories. We're trying to help people encounter the One who changes lives. Of course, teaching and telling stories is part of that, but we have to always keep Jesus in our focus. Speaking honestly, I've sat under a lot of great teaching in my life, but not until helping with the launch of our current church did we see what that could really look like. Everything must lead us back to relationship with Him.

This community, centered on Jesus, is then **commissioned to reach the world around us**. We are inviting people into this same place of encounter so that they can be transformed. Put another way, we are on a mission together. Our mission is to bring back His lost sheep, and to care for the ones we've found. I think many Spirit-filled believers have the same experience that Peter, James and John did on the mountain top with Moses and Elijah. They were so struck with the awesomeness of the encounter that they asked Jesus to "pitch a tent" up there so they could hang out in the glory indefinitely. Jesus, who lived a lifestyle of encounter, pointed them back down the mountain where the needs of the world around them were.

If I could go back and coach my younger self in our Cincinnati church plant with this definition, so much would have gone differently. First, the church is not primarily a personal fantasy-- it's a real gathering of people! You have to spend a lot of energy doing all of the practical things that it takes to gather people: inviting, holding events, special parties, getting the word out, etc. I needed to spend less time on the nuances of our statement of faith and much more time on how to bring people along with us.

*Our mission is to bring back His lost sheep, and to care for the ones we've found.*

Secondly, my heart as a pastor and my experience in heavy discipleship environments led me to be way too involved with people. If I had known how to walk with people at their own pace, instead of getting deeply involved and trying to push or drag them deeper, we would have avoided a lot of conflict, and some of the people who left would have stayed, and when people did leave it would have been a bit easier emotionally. This is a voluntary journey in every sense of the word! You only want people who want to be there.

As a Spirit-filled person, I thought I was pointing people to Jesus, but really I was pointing people to the Holy Spirit and all of the cool things He does. While it's essential to create a culture of hungering for more, the focus must always be revealing the *person* of Jesus – that is the purpose of all of the work of the Holy Spirit. I should have preached less about His power and desire to change the world, and spent a lot more time introducing and reintroducing all of us to how amazing He is, in all of life. If you haven't fully discovered that, don't start a church yet, but lean in and discover how He is the fulfillment of everything the 1 Corinthians 13 tells us love is. In my book *No Exit*, I try to unfold a bit of that.

Finally, I would have coached myself to "go out" a lot more. We needed to do things together as a church where we learned to enjoy each other, as well as things that were designed to touch and encounter people. You stepping out to be Jesus to the world always bears fruit even if you don't see the visible result of any particular activity. The church must be a place where you actually "go into all the world" including outreach and ministry to the community if you want to grow. This would have also included going virtually via all kinds of social media, which allows to encounter audiences in a virtual space, where more and more people are spending more and more of their time.

### TUNE TO YOUR DEMOGRAPHIC

Churches have a certain natural social dynamic as well. The general definition above ignores demographics, but most stable churches are built around stable families in the growing years. Families provide stability in many ways. First, they are easy to attract as many people with any religious background at all will tend to consider coming back to church when they are in the child-raising years. Secondly, once you have them if you do well, they are easy to retain as their children will keep them there. Thirdly, they have income that can sustain the church itself. Finally, a healthy family is socially cohesive – the health it has internally becomes the lifeblood of the church itself. This small nucleus of health and resources can begin to attract others and bring healing in all directions.

Based on my experience in campus ministry, urban ministry, nursing homes, and suburban ministry, I want to point out that building a church among demographics without stable families is very difficult. This is because of limited financial resources, less overall stability, and the continual need for significant ministry. Older people too, offer stability in comparison to youth, but are very hard to attract to a new church as they will usually stay in the church they are most comfortable in or where their children go.

This is not to say that you can't or shouldn't start churches in other situations, but you need to be aware of what you're getting into. You could, for example, build a church focused on younger people without children in an urban setting, but it is a unique endeavor, with a lot of turnover and requiring a kind of chic and social verve to keep the energy. If that is the kind of person you yourself are, you should definitely do so as it is always easiest to reach the people you are most drawn to.

Apart from a special calling and corresponding equipping to succeed in a unique mission, though, when you're thinking of starting a church, your default mode should be to bring in stable families as your core and then reach in many directions from there. This basic social structure is why certain things like a strong kids church and youth ministry are essential to success even early on. And if you are a male pastor, having your wife visible with you will help families connect to you better.

Every aspect of what you do has a hidden demographic message and audience to it. Tune to connect with who you are reaching. If you are reaching Marines at Camp Lejeune, you might want to preach hard do-or-die kinds of messages, but preaching to nursing moms and busy office dads that most do is an entirely different thing. Other churches that have already reached that demographic can give you ideas, so use that opportunity to network and get tips.

## A CHURCH MUST BE LAUNCHED

As a Spirit-filled leader who had pastoral education, I had a notion that if I brought the Holy Spirit and cared well for people, that my church would just grow organically on its own. In fact, it did grow somewhat through these means. However, one of the best observations of church planting professionals, which experience confirmed to me, is that organic growth is a very difficult way to grow a church . What you learn from a Systems perspective is that you have to grow it more like a flash mob! It's counterintuitive if you're thinking primarily in terms of pastoral care as I was, but it's true. You want to launch your new church, not just open the doors.

*You have to grow it more like a flash mob.*

The reason why you have to create a flash mob is both mathematical and social dynamics. Mathematically speaking, a smaller group has a much smaller capacity to grow and invite people. If everyone in a church of 50 invites someone and only 10% of them come, that's 5 new guests. If everyone in a church of 500 invites someone and only 10% of them come, that's 50 guests, but if only 1% of them come, that's still 5 new guests. Growth of any substantial amount is just too difficult when you're talking about ones and twos. Think about as a bank account. Growing from 50 to 100 dollars by collecting 5% interest would take you forever, but if you start with 500 dollars, adding that same 50 dollars is well within reach.

Socially speaking, small groups have the problem of a lack

of social space. When you have small numbers, your group is very tight knit and attracts people who are highly committed and also want to be in tight knit community, and a tight relationship with the pastor. There is less social space for different types of people in the group. The homogeneity that makes the smaller group feel fun to insiders also makes it feel uncomfortable to outsiders.

This means that a great deal of self-selection occurs as well. If the group grows a little bit, then the small dynamics fade, and the people who love small community leave, shrinking the group again. For these reasons, growing from a small group to a large church is incredibly difficult. A small community grown from scratch tends to maintain itself under 50, often smaller.

Another factor that plays into church growth is analogous to what happens to a house that goes on the real estate market. When a house is new, a rush of buyers comes to check it out. The longer the house stays on the market the more 'stale' it becomes and harder to invite people. Similarly, the more people that show interest in a house, the more likely there will be an offer or that the price will even go up. When a church is new, any pent-up demand in the city for a new expression will draw in new people. And as long as you are growing, the natural momentum will attract more people, just like a house in a buyers' market. However, once the new wears off or you lose momentum, it can be hard to regain. You have to shock the market to create a fresh breakout.

## BUILDING YOUR TEAM

To create the flash mob that launches your church, you have to start by gathering a large number of people all at once. For months, you build momentum by gathering your team and holding *interest meetings* as a kind of publicity. In between those interest meetings, you connect with as many people as possible to create momentum for the next meeting. When meeting with them, you cast vision for a big tent where they will all fit – essentially you are inviting them to be a part of the crowd.

Your team will probably not be who you think it will be. When we imagine starting a church, we usually think of our friends first, the people we have been dreaming with. The problem is that your friends are not your followers. They will have their own ideas and expectations about how things should go which will put pressure on both your friendship and the church plant. Starting a church with your friends is not generally a recipe for success. Your church is going to be built on followers – people who believe in you and your vision and want to follow you as you follow Christ (1 Cor 11:1).

Sometimes people who have a dream about authentic community or who have felt empty in large church settings will dream of a more "round table" structure, but this is also not a recipe for growth. You can have an enjoyable home group this way, but not a church. You will tend to spend all of your energy on relationships and negotiations about what to do next, instead of on growing and reaching out. This model of a single leader is also Biblical – from Abraham, to Moses to Jesus Himself, God changed the world through leaders and those who chose to follow.

**Get Sponsors.** Some of your friends may play a different role, however. Before you build a team of followers, you need people in your corner who are seasoned in ministry and who you trust to coach you to success. These people function like board members. They give credibility to what you are doing, help advise you in the process, and hopefully help you surface the financial resources you need to launch. They cheer you on and help you avoid pitfalls. If you don't have at least two independent people like that to lean on, you probably are not in a good position to plant a church. Leading and launching a church is incredibly taxing in many ways and presents a panoply of unique problems that no book could hope to catalog. That's why it's a team sport. No team on the field can win without a strong team of coaches helping from the sidelines.

**Cast Vision.** The key to building a team is to cast vision. Seek the Lord with your spouse and develop the vision you believe God is giving you. Of course, every church has a relatively similar vision to reach the lost, but yours will have its own unique spin. Building a successful church requires doing generic fundamentals, just like starting a business would, but your personal passion and identity make it unique and should draw people. Your unique vision, which should be an extension of your unique identity in the Lord, are what gives it life. Maybe you want to reach young professionals in the urban core of Denver, or build a fresh expression of the Holy Spirit on the north side of Orlando. Find the words.

Cast vision to the people around you that are most likely to follow you. Ask your friends and mentors who else might be warmly interested that they can introduce you to. This will hopefully mean lots and lots of coffee meetings getting to know people and looking for who might want to come on your adventure. Some of these will join your adventure, and others will help you through prayer and financial support.

**Core Team.** The purpose of this recruiting process to attract a core team. You are rolling a snowball – from these meetings, you want to be able to gather enough motivated followers to form a core team who want to build with you and are ready to work and if needed, move to help you launch. As you identify this core team, you should start to hold meetings with them and engage them in shared responsibilities to help build. Co-laborers are co-owners.

If you are not at a place where you have at least a small core of people who would follow you to a plant, you are not in a good position to plant a church. The easiest church plants are the ones where the leader has a large following already, and the hardest ones are where the leader has no following at all. Sometimes location is a part of this. Consider where you can go that you will be welcomed and celebrated.

It takes money to start everything, and a church is no exception. You need to put money in the bank to make all of this happen. If you can start putting the tithes of early adopters in the bank before launch day, that will help immensely. In addition, your board members, and other friends who may not choose to come along will often be thrilled to support you.

**Launch Team.** Around this core team who are doing the work to launch the church, you will build a launch team, and around that groups of interested people who want to join in. Your core team is in touch daily building momentum, and your launch team is the group of people around that. You are meeting with them weekly to worship together, pray into the coming launch, and build momentum toward the big day. These meetings are some of the most fun and exciting parts of a church plant. If you are doing it right, a holy expectancy builds as people are dreaming into what God will do. In between each meeting, you and your team are building momentum and a contact list of people who are interested in coming to a launch.

The pre-launch phase includes physical meetings and virtual presence. A lot of the world is virtual now, so you all need to be marketing, direct messaging and promoting what you are doing as much as possible. Your attractive but uncomplicated website should give people a way to plug in and build excitement. Everyone you meet should be added to an email list where they get updates and promotion every week. Your team should be creating and sharing social media posts which build expectancy for the coming launch. This will also connect you to friends of friends who you could otherwise have never met but want to be excited and join or even tell their friends!

## LAUNCH!

All of this activity creates momentum for launch. At this point you should have a strong virtual presence on social media, a great list of contacts and a general expectancy in the local community of the launch. Once you have these things, you are ready to press Go.

This means renting a space, picking a date, and using public marketing techniques to attract people you have never met before that aren't on your list. If you know a famous worship leader or other attractor, you can use this to sweeten the pot. Many church planters rely on renting public space for a launch and doing a lot of work to make it look more professional. The neutral space makes it an easy onramp for guests and renting allows you to be flexible for growth. Owning a building may seem attractive but the problem is it saddles you into a fixed size and fixed space, usually sub-par, with a lot of finances right off the bat.

Your goal on launch day is to start big. If you can get in the hundreds, you won't get caught in small church-churn. You want the social dynamics that larger groups provide. In addition to the traffic you have been building organically, consider at least one physical mailer to the community, as well as targeted social media buys. By getting the word out to a large number of people before the "big day," you can open with hundreds instead of with dozens.

Also keep in mind that while churches are planted to reach lost people, churches are not started *by* lost people. Your first set of people are going to be Christians who are looking for a fresh expression or a new church home. There is no shame in this. I see planting and growing a church as a creative process which will touch a lot of people in a lot of ways: people who have stagnated at their current churches and need a change, people who have become de-churched because their last church experience did not work out, and people whose state with the Lord is unclear.

This is real and valid ministry that we should not overlook or minimize. As you grow, it's normal that new attenders are believers from other places. As you build spiritual momentum, it becomes the kind of place that can sustain significant growth through revival and raw converts. Put another way, the nets have to be ready before the fish can come in. Other believers are a big part of that. Additionally, a great deal of good happens when you revive someone who has been hurt or stagnated in their walk. You are helping a branch that became unfruitful to become fruitful again.

Of course, once you gather these people, that presents its own challenges of sorting through who is there just to help you launch, who is really called to help you build long term, and who is just disgruntled from their last church. Your goal is to mobilize those believers who stay toward building a place of encounter where lost people are drawn in and transformed. Not all growth is people who are truly lost, but that is not a bad thing. As we target the lost we end up reaching a lot of other people as well, and if Jesus is in your midst He will use your church to accelerate their journey as well.

All of this will hopefully lead to hundreds of people showing up at your opening day, which is equally likely to drop-off considerably on week 2, so don't be discouraged. What you have on week 2 is your church, and if you steward it well, you will grow. The community is now of a size that it can be grown and sustained at a larger number—partly because of scale, but more fundamentally because of the social space created in larger groups for different types of people, and the faith that being in a larger group says they are "part of something." Now that you have people who are indeed part of "something," it is up to you to make that something into everything God has called it to be! In order to do this, we will turn to how people grow in relationship with God and how church systems accelerate that process.

# Building a Good System

## MARY OR MARTHA?

I would venture to guess that if you are a Spirit-filled believer like me you have heard countless sermons on Mary and Martha, in which Martha plays the villain and Mary the heroine. Martha stands for the people who are focused on work, and Mary stands for those who are focused only on extravagant devotion. Let's take a look at the story again:

> As Jesus and his disciples were on their way, he came to a village where a woman named Martha **opened her home** to him. She had a sister called Mary, who sat at the Lord's feet listening to what he said. But Martha was **distracted** by all the **preparations that had to be made**. She came to him and asked, "Lord, don't you care that my sister has left me to do the work by myself? Tell her to help me!"
>
> "Martha, Martha," the Lord answered, "you are **worried and upset about many things**, but few things are needed—or indeed only one. Mary has chosen what is better, and it will not be taken away from her." (Luke 10:38-42)

Thinking a bit about how sisters work, and also as a parent, it's not too hard to imagine this scene playing out. We can imagine Martha as a responsible older sister and Mary as a more carefree younger sister, and it's safe to guess that a version of this conflict had played out many times. So of course, it brought Martha to the breaking point when Mary started sitting at Jesus' feet during the visit. Mary, on the other hand, most likely lived as beneficiary of Martha's stewardship, which allowed her to be more carefree. And we can also guess that her highly responsible sister probably had a tendency to be in control and to over-prepare.

This story reminds me a bit of a Jason Upton meeting I went to once. The woman who hosted the event had done an amazing job turning the local civic center into a Garden of Versailles, complete with dozens of plants, figurines, tables and decorations. In fact, the decorations were so replete that it took a full team of people late into the night to unload them.

The setting was beautiful, people came, and Jason Upton gave the testimony of his adoption which was literally absolutely stunning. People were weeping uncontrollably. He was leading worship into a really deep place. But just as it was getting deep, the host team interrupted him in the middle of the set for some less important parts of the ministry. It was one of the biggest buzzkills I've ever seen in a ministry setting.

The hostess created the event in the hopes of hosting a powerful presence-oriented meeting, but when it came it was not honored properly. An overly massive effort went into the event – I'm sure a few plants would have done the trick, rather than a truckload—and little attention was given to the flow of the meeting where Jesus was expected to show up. The host team, like Martha, had become distracted from the purpose of the event, and almost killed the event by caring about the preparations and things to be done. It's not the preparations themselves that are bad, and certainly not the woman who put so much heart into the event, it's that these preparations allowed them to become distracted from the point of the event.

As we look more closely at the Scripture we notice that it was Martha who opened her home to Jesus. There would have been no visitation at all if there had not been a Martha. It required a Martha for Mary to have the encounter she had. Martha had simply worked herself up so much in the preparations that she missed the visitation, and not only did she miss the visitation, she got upset with her sister for attending it. She didn't get corrected for being a good hostess, or even for not paying enough attention to His presence. She got corrected for trying to take her sister out of His presence.

I tell this story because in the world of church leadership, just like in life, we need both elements. It's not Mary or Martha, it's Mary *and* Martha. Even the 24/7 prayer ministry of devotion to Jesus at IHOP requires schedulers to

> *It's not Mary or Martha, it's Mary and Martha.*

administrate, videographers to film it, a facilities crew, a security team, and every other support team. When we use this story to dismiss the role of administration and preparation we are actually undermining the very things we need to create the atmosphere for the Mary encounter

## FIX THE SYSTEM

For those of us who have had a powerful encounter with the Spirit, it's easy for us to believe that's all there is, but I've come to understand and see God as the Great Designer. The Holy Spirit doesn't work in spite of normal human social behavior, but with and through it. He is the Architect of the City that Abraham was looking for (Hebrews 11:10). We should sit at His feet to get the blueprints so we can build the city with Him!

The Holy Spirit does not work in spite of systems, He works through them. The Human Body is one of the most elaborate yet elegant systems ever designed, and that's because it's designer was God. If the church is the Body of Christ, then we should work with this master designer to create structures that, like the human body, allow life to flow.

In my younger years as a bivocational church planter, I spent my daytime hours in I/T as an Information Technology Architect, then a Business Analyst, and later a Project Manager. It was great mental training for analyzing how things work (or don't work) and what is needed to make them work. If the system is well-tuned, it will grow, and if it is not growing, there is something wrong. Interestingly, the Bible tells us exactly that:

> The whole body, joined and held together by every joint with which it is equipped, **when each part is working properly, makes the body grow** so that it builds itself up in love. (Eph. 4:16 ESV)

Paul compares the church to the human body, which, as every doctor knows, is an incredibly complex set of systems. When they are working well you experience the fullness of life, and when one is broken, you don't. That's what Paul tells us. So we need to do more than preach well, care well, or invite the Holy Spirit in order to grow. We know that's what *matters.* Yet we need to create systems that make the church body function properly.

*Your whole church is a system that is supposed to move people from non-believers to world changers.*

There are of course different ways to design and assemble the systems of the church, but at the most fundamental level, your whole church is a system that is supposed to move people from non-believers to world changers. This is not going to be accomplished overnight or through a single approach. It happens through a series of interlocking components that form a pathway of growth that someone can take with Jesus. Unfortunately, many churches have great experiences, but no pathway. For many churches, the system if it were to be drawn, would look something like this:

Personal Evangelism ➡ Worship Service ➡ Discipleship

Most pastors imagine that if they encourage their members to personally evangelize friends, family and co-workers, then they will bring them to a Sunday Service where they will then hear a great message, receive Jesus, and join whatever discipleship tactic we have in place. I say "imagine," because it rarely works that way.

Why not? The first reason is because most people rarely do any personal evangelism, especially if by that we mean

*Salvation may be an event, but evangelism is a process.* presenting the gospel to strangers or near-strangers. Secondly, when they do, the jump for most contemporary Americans to receive Jesus in the first place is quite large, and so is the jump to coming to a Sunday Service. Even if you do lead someone to the Lord while you're out and about, they rarely actually come to church for discipleship.

The fact that so few people do personal evangelism is not simply a sign of people's cowardice, it's also a reflection of ineffectiveness. If personal evangelism were more effective, people would do it more! People enjoy doing things that work and tend to avoid things that don't work, or things they feel they aren't good at. So in reality, in most cases, both the first box and the first arrow are missing from the above diagram. It's easy to see from that observation alone, why many churches do not grow.

## THE ENGEL SCALE

The Engel Scale is probably the most important insight in evangelism in the last 50 years. It's the recognition that not everyone outside the church is in the same evangelistic category. Instead, they are on a "scale" from overtly hostile to highly receptive to the gospel. Inside the church, not everyone is in the same place either. We exist on a spectrum from basic believer to world changer.

The idea of a scale is incredibly helpful when thinking about how to organize a church for effective outreach and growth. It helps us to think about evangelism in a fresh way instead of one-size-

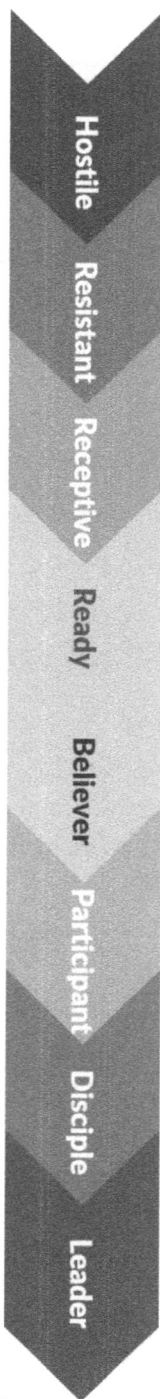

Hostile
Resistant
Receptive
Ready
Believer
Participant
Disciple
Leader

fits-all. We realize that different groups will need different tactics, and that moving someone along the path is a win to be celebrated. Salvation may be an event, but evangelism is a process. We should look at how to move people along the scale and seek to identify tactics that will address each different group well.

Since James Engel brought this idea into the mainstream in 1979 with his book *What's Gone Wrong with the Harvest* there have been many adaptations of this concept. So rather than present the scale itself, I'm going to present my own simplified version with a total of 8 phases. The first four phases are categories of non-believers adapted from Thom Rainer's *The Unchurched Next Door* which provides excellent insights into these groups.

**Hostile** – This is the person that most of us imagine when we think of "the world" or "the lost." This person is openly hostile to the gospel and may emotionally punish anyone who reaches out to them. The good news is that there are actually relatively a very small number of these people. We need to remind ourselves when we encounter them to pray for them, put a kernel of truth in, and then keep fishing where fish are biting.

Every once in a while, with fervent prayer, there will be an Apostle Paul to come out of this group, but it is extremely rare A look at the New Testament shows that many truly hostile people, like the High Priests, did everything they could to stop the gospel for as long as they lived. Prayer is probably the best offensive weapon here, as God is the One who moves in the secret places of the heart and asks us to love and pray for our enemies (Matthew 5:44).

**Resistant** – This person is not openly hostile, but they are not interested. If you have relationship with them, they will often show some level of value in your testimony because of their relationship with you, but they are generally not interested in Christianity. Oftentimes this is someone who has figured out how to make life work without God. They are satisfied with how things are and are not looking for answers. Or they have been raised with so much social distance and misperception of God, that it takes a long time to warm them up. This can also be a person who is comfortable in another religion. While we should definitely tell our testimony and invite them to appropriate events, we should not exhaust ourselves trying to wear down those who are resistant.

**Receptive** – A receptive person is open to the process that is going to lead them to Jesus. There is openness when you share, or curiosity. They ask you questions. They may even think they have a relationship with God already, perhaps from their childhood, family members who are religious, or from attending church themselves. They may be going through a season of shake up or transition that is causing a rethink in life. I believe that these are the people that Jesus has in mind when he said that fields were white unto harvest (John 4:35). These are the fish that are ready to bite! When we get radical about our faith we are tempted to look out and target the most vocal, hostile people yet there are huge numbers of people in the middle who are ready to come into the Kingdom if we will build the pathway and invite them down it.

**Ready** – This is the person we never imagine but need to focus on more: the person who is ready to receive the word with joy. All it takes is contact with the right believer in the right environment and they will meet Jesus. Every once in a while, you will meet them. This is the person who the Lord has been working on for some time. Maybe they have been through a life crisis, or maybe

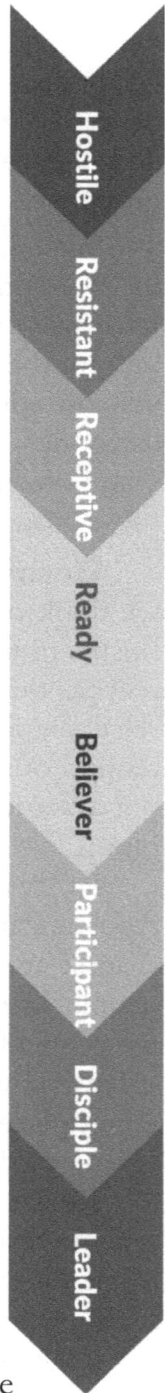

Hostile · Resistant · Receptive · Ready · Believer · Participant · Disciple · Leader

no one has ever paid any real attention to them. Maybe they are a late bloomer. You know you have met them because when you begin to talk about your faith, they light up and focus in. There's a hunger inside of them that is almost pulling the Word of God out of you. They are ready to meet Him.

The percentages of the population that are Hostile, Resistant, Receptive, and Ready vary within different regions of the world and changes over time, but all groups exist everywhere. Different constraints within society shuffle the percentages of who's in which category over time. Where your nation, state, or community currently is spiritually has a lot to do with factors which have come before.

In a culture or subculture where a large number of people are "ready," revival conditions can arise. Large numbers of people simply stream into the church as they hear the message in a way that is attuned to them. In places that are openly hostile, revival will look like smaller numbers of incredibly radical conversions because they had to jump so much social distance to accept Christ.

On the other side of the Engel scale are four more categories—this time, of believers who have accepted Christ. They are Believers, Participants, Disciples, and Leaders. Segmenting a population into the different Engel categories gives us a logical way to think about the needs of a congregation. We want to move people from the unreached side of the scale up towards leadership. Most people do not jump steps on the scale; rather, they progress through it. Each step takes time and specific tactics which are designed to reach people at each stage.

I am presenting an over-simplified view of these groups for the purpose of discussing how to grow a church. People in reality often exhibit a complex mix of maturity in some ways and need for growth in others. Also, I'm not suggesting that you actually use these four terms publicly – it could get weird, for example, if you label some people in your sphere as

"Disciples" but not others. But these categories are helpful ways to taxonomize Christian growth and commitment, that we need tactics to assist people through.

**Believer** – A believer is committed to Jesus and they are fellowshipping with you but that is the extent of their commitment at the moment. This is the largest group of people in the church. They are coming to be "warmed at the fire," but are not otherwise taking ownership of what is happening in the church or of their own growth as a Christian. If you are fostering a climate where Jesus is welcomed on Sunday, and people are being encountered, many of these believers are going to want to go further. Once they do, the key is to provide them avenues where they can take action on their newfound passion. As they become mobilized for Kingdom activity, it will lead to a multiplication effect.

**Participant** –A participant is a believer who has "come off of the sidelines" and wants to be actively involved in what God is doing. They are participating in the life of the church and looking for avenues where they can grow. Practically speaking, they serve on a team, help with a small group, or otherwise demonstrate their investment. Of course, everyone has life responsibilities outside of church which consume the majority of our time, but the participant has come to the place where they want to spend part of that time contributing to the life of the body.

These people are incredibly valuable and will grow into the pillars of the church if you steward them well. To foster the growth of participants, it's important to have on-ramps that provide easy opportunities for them to get involved not just to serve, but to grow in the knowledge of God. You need a pathway for them, readily available resources, and most of all a commitment from leaders to invest in them order to accelerate their journey and prevent them from being lost in the shuffle or shipwrecked by the enemy.

**Disciple** – A disciple is mature in their understanding of their faith, stable in their personal walk, and able to lead some part of your ministry with oversight. They are a participant who has been trained and established in the things of the Lord over time. Jesus' disciples went everywhere he did, and did what He told them and they had great fruit in this way. They were totally committed in every way to being transformed into His likeness, and to doing whatever it would take to see His Kingdom come

In order to produce disciples, it's not enough just to have some service opportunities and general teaching., you're going to need closer personal contact as well as higher intensity opportunities. They are going to have to walk closely with you and your other trusted leaders, where they can see your life. They are going to have to have their own adventures under supervision such as Jesus' disciples did when he sent out the 70 in pairs (Luke 10:1-24). The process of discipleship began for Peter when he threw down his net to follow Jesus, and it was completed at the cross. It took time and commitment.

**Leader** – Leaders are disciples who have grown to the place where they are capable of leading others. They are made in the furnace of serious obedience to the Lord. They have been through the storms of life and demonstrated that they will not be shaken. In the context of the church, a leader is someone who is building with you, and who probably has the capacity to build something on their own if they weren't. They not only have good foundations, but they are aligned to following you and building with you. The lives of others depend on them. They have capacity to follow well, but also the skill to build on their own.

In order to have a thriving church, you have to learn the art of not only developing leaders, but making room for them at the table. As a senior leader, you are limited by the caliber of leaders under you, therefore a good senior leader is always looking for people to reach their maximum potential, or their "leadership lid." We are trying to pull people up, rather than work them out.

One of the most common mistakes in ministry is not to make room for the growing "sons of the house." They must either be celebrated in the house or sent out with a blessing to establish their own ministry. Of course, this is a very difficult thing to do, which is why we don't see it done very often. The natural thing to do, even unintentionally, is to continue to work a productive person hard in their existing role or to disfellowship them as soon as they begin develop independent vision, but this will stunt their development as well as the growth of your own ministry. Of course, by the same token, sons often think they are ready before they actually are. The art of the dance is to give room for the Lord to lead.

## KINGDOM LEADERS

A word is in order here about what leadership really means. Leadership is not limited to just what happens inside the walls of your church, however. The church is an outpost of heaven which is commissioned to change the city. In order to change a city, the people of God must be bringing the presence and ways of God into daily life, the marketplace, where everyone is. No matter how amazing the encounters are inside our walls, they won't touch the world around us if we don't impact the culture. We are the salt of the earth and the light of the world. But when we when we fail to do this that we are "trampled by men." – that is the culture around us begins to persecute the church. The way we prevent this is by empowering and supporting leaders whose primary sphere of operation is not inside the walls, but outside. According to Ephesians 4:12, the full time office holders in the church sphere have the mission of "equipping the saints." Our goal is not just to produce more full time ministers, or part timers, but to equip the saints to change the world around us.

To be honest, it is the very rare church that understands this calling. It's common to feel like we've achieved success when people know how to do ministry, and to be so focused on the four walls that you can't see the direct value of

*The growth process does not stop inside the walls of the church.*

empowering people in the marketplace. That's partly because it is hard to run a successful church, and easy to get tunnel vision on what we're doing. In reality, the growth process does not stop inside the walls of the church. If we want to fulfill the mission of God in our generation, we must embrace and empower high-level leaders in both ministry and non-ministry settings. Consequently, they will bring a return back to your church in immeasurable ways. They are also the ones who will ultimately reach your city, which is on God's heart.

I'll never forget praying fervently for a young lawyer in our congregation when I was in college who was running for state Supreme Court. Not only did he win that election, we later went on to be the Chief Justice and finally Dean of a law school, doing many great things for the Lord along the way. We can only wonder what would have happened if we had not prayed and he had not received the support of the church in his journey. Of course, the larger congregation did not know the behind the scenes story, but as I have watched his career, I know that it all began with a church that believed not only in him, but in the importance of what he did outside the walls of the church.

True church success is marked by raising up leaders whose ownership of the Kingdom has grown and are leading others around them toward Jesus, both inside and outside the walls of the church. They have caught the vision that Jesus has come to change the world, not just gather believers, and have begun to partner with God to do that. They may run a Christian construction company, be a public office holder, or be a change agent in a professional context. I can only wonder how the current story of American history would be different if more churches understood the true broader mission of the church.

## CHURCH AS A BUSINESS?

As a person who has led in both business and in ministry, I have progressively discovered that growing a church and growing a ministry have many things in common: you have to generate leads for new business, convert those leads into clients, and retain those clients, so that hopefully those clients will produce referrals that grow your business.

Of course, I'm not the first person to have this insight, and so I want to make something very clear: the enterprise that we are embarking on inside the church is holy. While it has many similarities to secular business, it also has some fundamental differences. Failure to recognize the similarities will make it hard for you to grow it, but failure to recognize the differences will make it dry or even like a machine.

The most obvious danger of understanding this analogy is to treat "customers" like numbers on a spreadsheet instead of people. If people are buying tires, then things like margins and units sold are the most important measurements, but when you are dealing with people's souls, you're talking about something that has immeasurable worth. Jesus placed such a high value on a single life, that He sacrificed His own.

As soon as we lose sight of this, we've lost sight of our true mission. This means that we don't squeeze people for their money or their time to increase our "margins." We treat them with great worth and invite them to come along. To be honest, this is what well-run Kingdom businesses do too. The ones like Chick-fil-a that value their people more than their margins are the ones that succeed over the long run. It's no accident that their system produced a United States Senator. The value they have for people is felt from the moment you enter the door, or the moment that you start employee training.

A second similar mistake is to take the dry corporate language and experience that people are used to in the rest of life and try to model the church after it. I believe this mistake is most often perpetuated by leaders who have not spent any time in corporate spaces or who have managed to escape them for the fulfillment of ministry life. People come to church precisely because they want to escape the sterile language of the corporate sphere and experience authentic relationships, both with God and with each other. When people come to church, you goal is to create warmth and connection, and you have to communicate with people accordingly. Use the language of the God and you'll make disciples, use the language of friendship and you'll make friends, use the language of corporations and you'll have transactions.

## INSIGHTS FROM BUSINESS

Keeping the pitfalls in mind though, there is a great deal of clarity that can be gained by looking at the marketplace for insight. Business that work in a free market do so because they have tapped into Kingdom principles. The terms and systems that have been discovered there can be helpful to you and your leaders to focus and improve what you are doing. A leader of a church, you are not running a business in the sense of selling products to make money, but you are running an enterprise that is designed to attract people and help them grow. Your church converts human and financial capital into life change. Like a business, you must attract people, and serve them well so that they will grow and refer you to others.

Remember Pastor Tim who was cutting the grass at his small church? Like many small churches, he must do many things to simply keep the lights on, all of which seem important at the time. He was bogged down in all of these tasks and then confessed his sadness for not getting back with a man named Doug he had met through a divine appointment four weeks earlier. Tim had a background in business sales, and so I asked him, "If your church were a business and you were the CEO, which of these tasks would be most important?"

Immediately he realized that his most important job was to follow up with Doug. Someone else could cut the grass, or it could even go uncut, but a good CEO would never let a potential new client wait. Of course, you can argue that Pastor Tim should have known simply from his ministry convictions that he needed to follow up with Doug, but Tim had many important ministry duties. Understanding how his role was similar to the leader of a business helped give him the clarity he needed to take action. Later the next day he was standing in Doug's garage, talking about Jesus. A good CEO never stops making sales calls, and a good pastor never stops inviting people to come to church and meet Jesus.

You are the leader of an organization whose mission it is to bring people to Jesus, train them to do likewise, and then to change the world around you. If you don't understand this fundamental job role, you can do some great ministry, but you're not going to grow. If you primarily operate in pastoral functions, your people will receive care. If you primarily operate as a teacher your people will be established on firm foundations. If you primarily operate as an evangelist, lost people will meet Jesus for the first time. If you primarily operate as a prophet, people will amazed and touched by tidbits from heaven. But none of these functions by itself is going to cause a church to grow.

Although your traditional title is "pastor," building a growing church means you must function in the apostolic role of marshalling all of these kingdom functions toward building a growing body. You must learn to think like a builder. You are building a pipeline that starts with the lost, and leads to leadership, and must have every step in between. Any part of that pipeline that is broken or does not exist will prevent you and the people you are called to serve from reaching their destiny.

## HOW ORGANIZATIONS GROW

Perhaps the most important analogy to the world of business is what is called a "sales funnel," pictured in the diagram below:

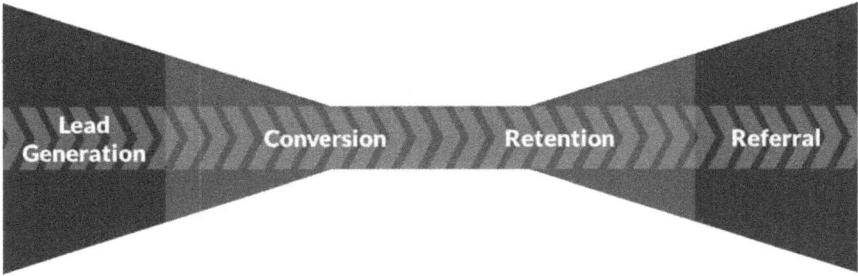

The sales funnel depicts the phases that a client moves through in their journey with you. They start as a lead, they convert to a customer, and hopefully they are retained. The left side of the funnel shows that there are always more leads than there are conversions. As the level of commitment increases, the number of people willing to make it decreases. Any business that is doing these four phases well will grow, and any business that has one or more of these components broken will struggle.

On the other side of the picture, the funnel widens again to show the increasing impact you can have as people become more committed believers in what you're doing. Every client that you serve well leads to ongoing value and to potential new clients as they refer you to others. Or put another way, the more strongly they believe in your product, more people they will tell about you.

If we were to translate this idea into Christian functions we need to build in our church, then we could have something like: Outreach, Encounter, Growth, Ministry, and Leadership.

Each portion of this funnel is a phase of growth which needs its own set of interlocking tactics – its own system – to effectively help people along the journey. The marketing end of your church generates interest, which should be done widely, fewer will encounter Him and choose the path of growth. Once they do, however, they can yield 30, 60, or 100 fold. (Mat 13:8). Churches that are growing have systems in place which perform these functions well. The stronger and more life-giving the systems, the more the church will grow. If you want to grow your church, reach the lost, and change your city, then the key is to build systems which address each of the steps along the way.

The **Outreach** System will be designed to put us in contact with people who we currently do not have contact with, so we can begin to bring them into the Kingdom. The **Encounter** System will help people who we know come across the threshold from darkness to light. **Growth** will aid believers in getting engaged in church life and activate their faith. **Ministry** is a system for helping people get their needs met as well as meet the needs of others. Finally, the **Leadership** System will move people from helping others to leading others in all of the other systems and endeavors of life. Your growth pathway is designed to generate "customers" from your leads, and then channel them into purchasing what you and your church is "selling."

Because, if you think about it carefully, the "sale" you are trying to make is the biggest sale of someone's life. It's bigger than a house or a car – it's their life itself. It's not a simple transaction, it's a sacred trust. Any salesperson will tell you that the bigger the sale, the longer the sales cycle. Which doesn't mean we never make quick conversions, but that you should plan and be prepared for people to have a reasoned and thoughtful process of life change, rather than a straight-to-video testimony. People who sell relatively small things like vacations or even cars can get away with being pushy, but anyone who has ever worked a big corporate account, or asked money from a major donor will tell you that being pushy is the quickest way to never be invited back.

This idea of the "long sell" can be a hard concept to swallow for some of us because we are raised and fed on dramatic testimonies. That's a self-fulfilling prophecy, though. When dramatic testimonies happen, those are the ones we choose to tell! We don't usually tell stories about the multi-year outreach process to a de-churched neighbor. Those sound boring to us because they are much more common. Alternatively, many times we don't know about the "long sell" that went on before the big decision, so it doesn't make it into the story. We can end up with a biased perspective of how God really works.

This causes us to miss a huge portion of the market though, the part that is "boring" and "much more common." That part of the market is *most* ready: people who are in many ways just like us but haven't met Jesus yet. Remember the person you are most likely to reach is the person who is most like you. This is why world missions has progressively come to focus more on empowering native missionaries – because they can reach their own people best. This doesn't mean we never go cross culturally, but our first harvest should be in our own backyard. You and your congregation are native missionaries in your local community.

Furthermore, we sometimes miss the other side of the funnel and the possibilities that exist there. People are always the greatest resource of any organization, and people who are already part of your church are far and away your greatest resource. If you train them well, they will bear fruit, some 30, some 60-, and some 100-fold.

## CONCENTRIC CIRCLES

While there are similarities, one of the fundamental differences between sales in the marketplace and church growth is the fact that we are building a *community*. We are inviting people to progressively deeper levels of connection and commitment. Therefore, we could look at their progression in terms of concentric circles. As people deepen and grow in their walk with God, they move into the more central regions of your church community.

This was one the elements that enabled Rick Warren to build such a large church—he built systems with the recognition that that Jesus had different layers of closeness around Him. He had *crowds* that followed Him, He had *seventy* committed disciples that He trusted to send out with His message, He had *twelve* handpicked apostles to govern the church when He left, and He had *three* intimate friends. Each of those layers of intimacy had differing levels of access to Him, participated in different activities, and even received different messages. Thus, if you look at growth from a social angle, you might have something like the picture below. [2]

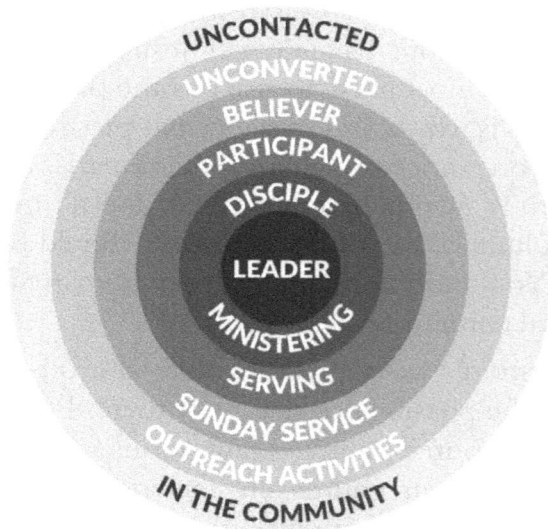

Does this look familiar? The ministry of Jesus had concentric levels of fellowship very similar to the way the Tabernacle had concentric levels of encounter. It's not an exclusively Old Testament or New Testament principle, it's a timeless aspect of how God brings people from lost to found.

On the outer circle, you have people that are "uncontacted." You do not know them, and they do not know

---

[2] This diagram is adapted from the *Purpose Driven Church* to fit this book.

you. That's the non-believers in your community at large. In order to bring this group in, you will need specific strategies geared toward contacting them, including events, small groups, and other forms of outreach.

Just inside that ring are those who have some touchpoint with you. This could be through existing relationships, or it could be from one of your outreach activities.

Inside the next circles you have increasing layers of growth for the individual believer. Each step along the path needs its own tactic to bring people inside it, and it also needs a message properly tuned to who is there, and their next logical step.

The reality of the concentric circles is what makes a lot of church life feel shallow to people that have been in the Lord for many years. The "milk" is for great crowds, but the stronger the "meat" you serve, the smaller the circle you have. There are a few places which are exceptions to this rule, i.e. IHOP, Upper Room, or Bethel. There, deeper messages are consistently preached to all levels.

These churches consequently function as equipping centers for the entire Body of Christ with world-class leadership that attracts people from around the globe. If you have this level of gifting as well as the mandate of heaven, you might be able to replicate their model! But for most of us, running a church of any size means finding the sweet spot which can edify the outer circles while creating systems which draw people into the inner circles.

Each of these layers of community serves a different purpose to someone who is at a different place on their journey. In Jesus' day, the crowds came for bread and for a kind of holy entertainment—they were on the outer ring. But Jesus' friends came because they loved Him and were committed to Him. They were on the inner rings, with different motives than those outside. If we map these rings onto the various parts of the church, we get the table below:

| Group | Where They Are | Place to Invite Them | System to Touch |
|-------|----------------|----------------------|-----------------|
| Uncontacted | In the Community | Outreach Activities | Outreach |
| Unconverted | Outreach Activities | Sunday Service | Encounter |
| Believer | Sunday Service | Next Steps | Growth |
| Participant | Serving | Joining Groups | Ministry |
| Disciple | Leading in the Church | Leading Groups | Leadership |
| Leader | Leading in the City | Leadership Meetings | Leadership |

As you can see, each of layer of the community circle has its own specific set of tactics including a community component. These are systems. Through these systems, the person is therefore continually invited to take the next step into deeper commitment. Each of the five systems is designed to reach a different person at a different point in their walk, yet connect them together in a realistic growth pathway through your church.

# The Outreach System

## THE PROBLEM OF MODERN EVANGELISM

Most people understand evangelism to be when someone gives their verbal testimony to a non-believer and invites them to pray a prayer of salvation. Maybe you don't hold this idea, but there is a good chance many people in your congregation do. It's a holdover from a bygone era of evangelism when a great deal of the evangelism was about introducing nominal or cultural Christians to the real Jesus.

The problem facing the church when Christianity held cultural sway was helping people see that they needed a living encounter with Jesus, not simply to be a good churchgoer. Accordingly, the church focused a great deal of its message and energy toward the kind of messages that would awaken people who had a false sense of security.

But we are now in an increasingly cross-cultural era when you are safe to assume that whomever you are talking with is not a believer and has never been one. They may not even be familiar with true Christianity. Under normal circumstances, this kind of person has to first be introduced to the gospel progressively, starting from whatever perspective they have.

I think it's a little like the first time I went to a Starbucks. When it first came out, Starbucks was not simply a new coffee shop but a new culture. I needed to learn entirely new vocabulary like the fact that a "grande" was actually a medium while a "venti" was a large. I felt very out of place because I was dressed different from most of the people there. To be honest, it took me several years to not feel weird whenever I went in. I was a Dunkin Donuts coffee guy years before I set foot in a Starbucks. It took maybe ten years before I knew what a barista was. And this was just my process buying coffee!

You can only imagine therefore what a non-Christian goes through when they enter church. We need strategies that lower the barrier. I bet I might have gone to Starbucks sooner if they had brought their coffee to places where I felt safe, like my office or a grocery store. It's not a big jump at all to see how that applies to growing a church or to receiving Jesus. This is the true definition of "outreach."

In addition, with the increase of portable entertainment technology and urban lifestyle, people are less open to in-person conversation with a random stranger than we were before. We assume people wanting to talk to us randomly have an having an agenda. We are pre-conditioned to say no even before they start talking. Think about how you reacted the last time someone came to your door to sell something—yet some segments of the church still push this as the best and only way to reach others.

This is a kind of a cod-liver oil theory of Christian outreach. Back in the old days, your grandma would give you cod-liver oil, which was disgusting and foul smelling, in order to help you with any number of maladies. That fact that it was disgusting had a strange psychological effect, however—people believed that it was working exactly because of how foul it was! This is sometimes how we act about evangelism. We have this idea that you should do it exactly *because* it is hard and uncomfortable for everyone involved, and if you don't want to do it, it's because you aren't enough of a Christian. This leads to a confrontational style of evangelism which is only well-suited to confrontational people—exactly the kind of people we don't want to represent us in most cases. We become telemarketers for Jesus! And just like telemarketers, people learn to despise us and also what we represent.

One way to think about effective outreach in this modern age is, "What would it take for me to convert to Mormonism?" Now of course, as church leaders, the idea is inconceivable right from the start, but that's actually where a lot of our target audience is starting from as well! So, for just a moment, hold that thought, and consider what it might take to move you.

Would you give a Mormon missionary the time of day at the door? Probably not. Would you have a conversation with someone on the street about their faith? Again, no. Would you let a co-worker talk to you about his Mormon faith? You probably would if he were polite and relational, or it had some practical relevance to something going on in life. But under what circumstances would you go visit a Mormon event? At a Mormon church? Now that's a higher bar, isn't it? Would you do it if a family member who died was Mormon? Yes, most people probably would. Would you do it to hear the Mormon Tabernacle Choir? Some Christians would for sure. What if you were deeply moved by a message or service...would you consider going back? You might not, but what about someone in your congregation?

Thinking about being evangelized gives us good insights on how we should approach evangelizing others. You can see that the stronger the relational connection, the more likely you are to become open to at least having a dialogue. Also, you are much more likely to go for a special event than to a regular service. The good news is that as the old adage goes, "No one wants to be sold, but everyone wants to buy." Instead of pushing people to close a deal, we should be inviting them.

Similarly, under what circumstances would you go *do* something with a group of Mormons? Would you ever go to someone's house to study the Book of Mormon? Very doubtful. What about a study of *The 7 Habits of Highly Effective People*—written by Stephen Covey, who is Mormon? Actually, that's quite possible. The topic and the pretext for getting together matter as well, don't they? And once you are in relationship or comfortable hanging around the Mormon community, you are much more likely to take further steps in that direction.

When you think about this, you start to realize that "inreach" is actually outreach. Inviting people to "come in" to participate in what you are doing is one of the most effective ways of reaching out. If the Mormons can get you to come see the Mormon Tabernacle Choir, they have already taken you several steps toward being evangelized. You've moved from hostile to at least mildly open.

In the same way, bringing people into contact with a healthy family of believers creates a bridge they can cross to find Jesus. The first part of the gospel that we know so well from Matthew 28 is to "go and tell," but the other part is to invite people to "come and see." Remember the story of the woman at the well? After the woman at the well had a supernatural encounter with Jesus, she told all of her friends to come saying:

> **"Come, see** a man who told me everything I ever did. Could this be the Messiah?"** (John 4:29)

This woman had a touch from Jesus and then became the lead coordinator of a community event where Jesus was the featured speaker.

The Queen of Sheba had a similar experience, except no one specifically went to tell her at all. She came strictly based on the power of referral and reputation:

> When the queen of Sheba **heard about** the fame of Solomon and his relationship to the LORD, **she came** to test Solomon with hard questions… The report I heard in my own country about your achievements and your wisdom is true. But I did not believe these things until I came and saw with my own eyes. Indeed, not even half was told me; in wisdom and wealth you have far exceeded **the report** I heard. (1 Kings 10:1,6)

What was going on at Solomon's court was so amazing that people were talking about it, which led the queen to go see it for herself. When she did finally make the journey, she was awestruck. We know from Jesus' prophecy that she was also converted by the encounter she had:

> The Queen of the South will rise at the judgment with this generation and condemn it; for she came from the ends of the earth to listen to Solomon's wisdom, and now something greater than Solomon is here. (Matthew 12:42)

If Solomon living in the Old Testament could build his Kingdom in such a way that a queen would travel a thousand miles from her kingdom to see it, and then be converted by it, then we can do even better if we host the presence of Jesus. The one "greater than Solomon is here," with us (Matt. 12:42).

### BUILDING AWARENESS

Putting this together, we can think about the Outreach System as having several components or sub-systems: Building Awareness, Events, Outreach Groups, and Personal Outreach. Let's look at the first, on how to build awareness.

In Romans 10:14, Paul highlights some of the process of evangelism when he says:

> But how can they call on him to save them unless they believe in him? And **how can they believe in him if they have never heard about him?** And how can they hear about him unless someone tells them? And how will anyone go and tell them without being sent? (Rom 10:14-15 NLT)

One of the things Paul points out is that people must first *hear* about Jesus before they can believe in Him. In business speak, this is what is called **raising awareness**. People must know about your product before they can even think about buying it. They must usually hear about it several times before they even notice it.

John the Baptist had an entire ministry of raising awareness! He did not perform any miracles that we know of or build any structures, but went out into the desert, lived the prophetic lifestyle, and then began to baptize and call people to repentance, telling them to be ready for the coming of the Lord. By the time Jesus came, people were ready to receive the message he had because of the ministry of John the Baptist.

What is our John the Baptist ministry in the 21st century? How do we build awareness of Jesus, the real Jesus in our culture? There are people who do not come to your church who have some awareness of your church, and for whatever reason they are not coming. But what about people who have not heard about your church? Some of these people would come, if they were to simply hear about it.

In the technological world, this phenomenon has been observed as the adoption curve. For any given product, such as the iPhone, it looks like this:

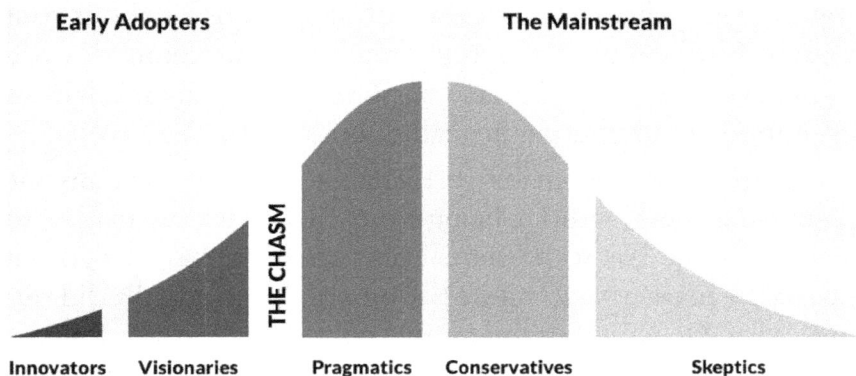

**Early Adopters**                    **The Mainstream**

THE CHASM

Innovators    Visionaries        Pragmatics    Conservatives          Skeptics

Most people know someone who is iPhone-crazy who always has the latest version and proclaims the next release date with all the upcoming features. This is the "early adopter" or enthusiast – ready to do the next great thing. Right next to that person are those who will definitely upgrade as soon as possible. These people form a small portion of the total population but create social momentum.

If the product lives up to expectations, it will break across "the chasm" in into the mainstream. People who barely care about phones at all will start to adopt the iPhone because they don't want to be left behind. Skeptics of course will hold out until the last possible point if possible, but some of them like my wife will eventually be won over as well.

Your church builds momentum the same way. There are some people who are ready to come right now who just haven't heard about it. Innovators and visionaries are going to come just because they are excited that something new is happening. These pioneering people may be with you for only a season, as they are the kind of people who love to start and be part of the next great thing, but they are essential to building momentum and getting you across "the chasm" that separates you and the mainstream.

If you can break into the mainstream, large numbers of untapped people suddenly become available to you. As your influence and reach grows, if you're doing well, you hit a tipping point where almost everyone at least knows about your church. If it gets big enough like the big name ministries you know, eventually people have to start defining themselves as *not* going to your church, instead of going!

At the end of Romans 10:15 Paul says, "how will anyone go and tell them without being sent?" In order for people to hear, someone has to be sent. This means we have to go out into to the marketplace where people are. Jesus actually did this quite a lot. He taught in the temple courts, the center of public life, so often that the Pharisees knew where to find Him. Paul did similarly, teaching and preaching in synagogues and gathering places.

Of course for us a great deal of that marketplace now is virtual rather than physical. We have to be "sent" into these virtual spaces where people spend most of their time. Awareness is anything and everything you can do to let people know you exist. With that is creating a favorable impression of who Christians are as a community of believers. As mind-bending as it might be, your marketing director may be the most important evangelist in your church.

### MARKETING

Marketing your church simply means doing the things that are designed to get your message across to a target audience. These are the kinds of things you would do no matter what you were building or starting because you want to get your message out. There are many people who are professionals at this who can help you – and in fact you probably even have people in your church with a great deal of skill in these areas. Make use of their skills; don't let them sit on the sidelines.

Remember that people have to see something *many* times before they even register that they have seen it. Marketers will tell you this is because we train ourselves to block information out. Some marketers say we have to see something seven times, and some say even more in the digital age before we register that we know about a product or service. The beauty of understanding the awareness-building process is that it takes pressure off of you to "close the deal" every time you encounter someone. You simply have to make your presence known to build your church and reach people. Everyone can do that!

One of the first things to consider is your location. Now of course, you may not be in a position to change locations, but it is still one of the most important variables in getting your name out there. This is why you will notice that many newer and larger churches occupy buildings that look more like a store than a church, and are located in places that are highly accessible and visible. Having the building be physically visible helps people know you exist, which helps them think about coming. Maybe this just means some tree pruning!

Right with this, is your sign. You want a prominent and well-placed sign, and maybe a tagline that people can think about when they drive by, like "A place to find hope" or "We believe in second chances." In addition, placing banners closer to the road or flag signs out on drive-by areas on Sunday will greatly heighten awareness. Many prospective attendees are out and about on Sunday morning and will see your sign every time—perhaps prompting them to give it a try. Most of the time people need an invitation to set foot inside the door, but sometimes seeing a sign over and over again is enough. This is especially effective for our church which meets in a school. We don't have our own building yet but we do have a whole team that advertises our presence on Sunday mornings.

The second part of marketing is your virtual location– your web page. What does your web page say about you? By that I mean, what impression does it leave on people who visit it? If someone drove by the church and then Googled it, would what they encounter online that would make them more or less likely to come?

*The average person sizes up their options visually before they go deeper into content.*

As leaders trained in the Word of God, we tend to focus heavily on content given *in* church at the expense of impressions people have before or upon arriving at church. Yet the average person sizes up their options visually before they go deeper into content. What kind of images do you have online? What are the key messages, both conscious and subconscious, that people will get from what you have put out there? What reviews will they read, or will there be none?

After the web page is the overall online marketing strategy. Online marketing is incredibly intelligent now. It allows you to micro-target small areas and demographics. You can have your church pop up on Facebook or Instagram only among people with some affinity for church messages, or only in results on Google related to God-oriented searches. This allows you to raise awareness among your exact target audience at the exact time you want them to know about you. In addition to ads, your Instagram feed is like a continual advertisement. If a seeker gets as far as looking at your church, you want them to see friendly people there and the great time they are having. Take a look at any large and successful church for ideas of what this can look like.

It's great to have a marketing and online guru in your community, but it's not just the job of someone in the office to do this. In the current era social media is how we "tell our friends" that something great is going on. My brother visited me recently and he took a picture of us, a picture of the food, a picture of the kids, and then shared them all. All of his friends and even acquaintances saw the fun we were having. The same is true of you, your team and your church members. As mind-bending as it may sound to many people at first, part of reaching today's lost is people sharing on social media. Personal evangelism may be harder in our media world, electronically initiated forms of personal interaction, such as chatting with an Uber driver or even meeting a potential date online, are actually easier. We learn more from online media than ever before, and may quietly reconsider our deepest held convictions after a great video or podcast. Unbelievers will also get input from your images, even if they'd never ask you a question up front. This means what we share virtually is a key part of our evangelism.

Of course, this has to be natural, not overblown. If you push your team to share every single post your church does, their friends will shut them off just like they do with their friends selling shampoo. The pastor will have more flexibility in this area because people expect that you will be representing the church all of the time – you are the brand. Train a team and empower your congregation to share what they are doing with your church on social media in organic ways. Help them make the connection to how they are reaching lost people.

Another important and even easier way to engage your congregation in awareness building is through branded merchandise or "swag." Most businesses and large ministries are aware of the power of swag, but the church is only slowly understanding its power. When you put someone into a t-shirt that has the name of your church on it, you turn them into a walking awareness campaign.

You might also find that when you're wearing an advertisement, the conversations you need to have can start themselves! When I am out and about in my city wearing the gear for our church, it is not uncommon at all for me to end up in a conversation about it. Our church has a continuous campaign of designing logo merchandise "merch" and giving it away to people who participate in different activities like community service day. People love the stuff, it serves a great purpose in building awareness, and it also helps people to feel part of a community. Swag is a small investment that's well worth it, and many options are available by print-on-demand so you don't have to overbuy or plan months ahead.

Then of course there is still traditional paid mailing to your target audience. One of the ways our church launched with a large number of people was by direct mailing a huge number of people to invite them to come. You can target your neighbors pretty specifically with a postcard campaign to let them know you are there, or are holding a charity event. Paid physical mail is an essential part of launching a church but can also be helpful when you want to invite fresh faces—taking advantage of the holiday season or new year, for example. It's costly but still very effective. Although most people will only look at an advertisement for a few seconds on the way to the trash, it starts the awareness process.

## AWARENESS ACTIVITIES

Over the years, our family has become aware of many churches' existence that we have never driven by. Our local Catholic parish, for example, does a visible food drive that many people on our street participate in. They also encourage their schoolchildren's families to put a small sign in their front yard which advertises where they attend. Because of these things, I'm aware of their church even though I couldn't tell you the name of most other churches in our area.

Most of the time when we think about going out into the community for the purpose of evangelism, we're thinking of something very direct. But when we put on the mindset of building awareness, the pressure goes down a lot and it becomes something fun that everyone can do.

For example, you could pay for a booth at a local festival where you pray for people or give things away. God can open specific and natural doors to invite people to church, pray for their healing or give them the gospel, but by putting the focus on just being known in the marketplace, you aren't forcing that to happen. It's pretty easy to approach organizers of local events like 5-Ks or parades and ask them to host a prayer station from your church where people can receive prayer for needs. By doing this, you're creating a scenario your whole church can participate in, as well as putting your name out in the public sphere.

*If you have your own church facility, think about how you can use it to bring the community to you.*

Or, if you have your own church facility, think about how you can use it to bring the community *to you*. This can be outreach and in-reach at the same time. The Presbyterian church near me allows their facility to be used as a polling station. This means I actually set foot in their church building at least once a year. In fact, most of the people in my neighborhood do as well. While this could be seen as a hassle by many church leaders, there is a great deal of value to becoming a place that people are just comfortable coming to—simply because they've set foot in the door for other purposes.

You might lend your church to a nearby neighborhood association that needs a place to meet, or a support group, a Cub Scouts troop, a local event, etc. My friend hosts a state-funded daycare at his facility. He uses this as a continual ministry to the community, and this year has taken the step to give Christmas gifts to the underprivileged children enrolled there. The unreached are coming to him simply because of how he uses his building!

You can also engage the civic arena to build awareness. Political officials are always looking for touchpoints with the community. You can even do this in a way that is non-political. For example, giving the invocation at civic events such as the town council meeting creates legitimacy for your church. We once had a pastor who would go into the office of every newly elected official and offer to pray with and for them. This led to the County Manager joining his church! Another friend of mine gives each official an attractive copy of the Ten Commandments. These kinds of activities give you the opportunity to influence leaders and the city at large, but they also help make your church a visible part of the community. Think about it as involvement, engagement, and awareness rather than stereotypically "political."

Remember, awareness building is not about closing a deal, but starting one. God can and will use your awareness building at any later point. My wife and I joined a church of a pastor we saw once at a citywide prayer event. He was shocked that we had heard about him that way, but his two minutes on the microphone at the meeting created awareness that we pulled on when we were ready.

## EVENTS

Some people will visit you on Sunday just as a result of awareness building, but then most will need a second step, which is **invitation**. This can be in-person by a church member, or via physical mail, an online campaign, or other intentional avenue.

What should they be invited to? Remember the Mormon example: you are much more likely to go see the Mormon Tabernacle Choir than you are to attend a service at the local Mormon temple. You have to create easy on-ramps for people if you want them to come into your community. Christians who are already looking for a church will come to a random Sunday service, but for the unchurched this could be a big step, several points later in the chain. Creating and leveraging opportunities where there are easier points of entry is key.

The first things to leverage are "big days" for your church. This means creating a special event out of your service, the most obvious being Christmas and Easter. Christmas and Easter are special because people who do not otherwise come to church will show willingness to do so, or simply accompany others by ritual. Congregants invite friends and family who are often willing to come just because of the holiday.

For this reason, it is important to make every effort to leverage these built-in events. Have a choir or pageant, or a candlelight service so that people who are looking for a special experience can find it at your church. Then believe God for the Holy Spirit to touch them, and make them feel so welcomed that they want to come back again. Give them that invitation directly. Engage your congregation on a mini-campaign to invite those in their sphere to these kinds of services. For us inside the church, we feel every day is as important to God as Easter or Christmas! But for those outside, it is probably one of the only times their minds are naturally open to Christian beliefs and reflection.

You can create other kinds of events which are easy on-ramps as well. During the summer, a church picnic can become an easy way to invite friends and neighbors. Special speakers can be a great invitational event to motivate the congregation to invite others. Marriages and funerals are event put on by others for a purpose outside the church but are natural to leverage as a hidden doorway into the church. My wife's unsaved family started to attend the church that we were married in, simply because the church said "yes" to holding the wedding. He got an invitation he couldn't refuse!

Organizations use **events** to build momentum and create new connections between people. Even though they take a lot of effort, when used properly they can catapult an organization or even an entire market forward. The same is true within the church. Harness the power of events in order to grow. Events operate like a spring – you do a lot of work to load it with energy, and then when you release it, it can catapult you forward. But *only* if you leverage the power of the event. And the invitation process.

After you put in all the energy to create a friendly environment, and get people there, don't leave opportunities on the table by not connecting and following up with them! Assemble a small team to greet, make connection cards, and then touch back. Consider having a small business card, special gift, or thank you that visitors can take home with your information on it. This is probably the hardest part to do, but it is important because it is the last touchpoint with your new potentials. On your end you feel as if you're closing the deal, but on their end, you are opening it.

Many pastors already do this on Sundays. The Sunday service is of course your first and most important event. It happens every week. You and your team put a tremendous amount of energy into it. Make sure to create and leverage every possible opportunity it presents to connect with people who gathered there. This means you and your team should work the crowd look for new faces, and connect with guests. Every guest that passes by without making a connection is a lost opportunity, one that you put a lot of work upstream into making happen. Don't miss it!

This is something you'll likely have to practice and coach your team to do. Instead of standing around talking to each other, during the Sunday you should work in a coordinated fashion to ensure that no one slips through the cracks. It's easy to get bogged down just talking to each other, but remember there will always be more time to talk to friends. If you don't talk to your guests, this is likely the only time you'll ever see them. Most people who return to a church do so because they felt authentic love and connection from the people that are there. On the other hand, feeling a lack of connection is the most common reason for people to leave.

### OUTREACH GROUPS

Beyond special events, your church needs **small groups** that have an outreach-oriented focus. These will be different than small groups for other purposes. By nature, any group you

*What feels safe to an insider feels exclusive to an outsider.* create will naturally focus on itself, which is great for fellowship but bad for outreach. What feels safe to an insider feels exclusive to an outsider. Therefore, if you want outreach to happen through small groups, you have to intentionally create it.

The ideal outreach group is one that connects with people in a space that is safe to *them*. It offers them a piece of community outside the walls of the church. An example of this would be a sports or hobby-themed group. If a man in your church loves golf and invites some friends from church as well as other people he knows, you have created a perfect connection between believers and non-believers.

My experience is that the best people to charter this are those who may not actually be the strongest disciples in your church! We once had a man in our church who did not seem really ready to take deeper steps in his journey with the Lord, and I really didn't know what to do with him. As we talked, I realized he was a huge fishing and outdoors fan. I told him to invite his friends to an outdoor men's weekend, and my associate and I would love to come and participate. When we went on the retreat, he brought a bunch of unsaved family members and unchurched friends. We held a campfire service and prayed for each of them—*and they all got saved or took a step in their faith*. Now it was nearly impossible to imagine this unchurched group coming to our church service. But when we went with them into their community, they were more than comfortable and happy to have us there. More importantly, they responded to the Lord!

This, I believe, illustrates the best way to charter small outreach groups – as a partnership between people who are highly capable ministry leaders and those who might seem to be less committed or are earlier in their journey. The fact is, ministry leaders often don't have a lot of hobbies or friends outside the church because the things of God have become their hobby. Most of them have very little time. This makes it difficult for them to have great outreach groups by themselves. By the same token, those who are more connected to worldly people can bring those people in and benefit from having a leader there with more ministry capacity. By pairing the two together, you can create a bridge.

## PERSONAL OUTREACH

The foundation of outreach hinges on individuals in your congregation being able to reach and touch the people around them. If you're a pastor, however, your social network is probably larger than most people's in your church but also more insular. You will tend to be surrounded by people who have already been reached, not those who still need to be reached. So, one step is simply creating some intentionality about being outward facing with your own life activities. In every organization, the leader must be the chief salesperson and promoter or the organization will stagnate. You are the role model that everyone else will follow. If you are not reaching out in some way, most of them won't either.

*We are doing things to bring others in contact with the love of Jesus that is inside of us.*

On the other hand, when your entire church is an evangelistic system, there are many ways for you and everyone around you to participate in evangelism. What matters most is that people internalize this value. We are not just doing things we like—we are doing things to bring others in contact with the love of Jesus that is inside of us. We share our great moments on our Instagram feed because we want people to know about Jesus. We host a dog-walking small group because we want people who walk their dogs to meet Jesus. We serve and help run big events because those are times that people can come meet Jesus for the first time. We smile and welcome others because that's who Jesus is inside us, and He needs to be seen.

*Friendship evangelism* was a major concept for a long time, and seen as an alternative to personal witnessing. It is the concept of befriending non-believers with the purpose of reaching them. The key observation behind this concept was that people are much more open to their friends sharing Jesus with them, than they are in hearing from a stranger. While this is certainly true, I think the logical conclusion most people reach when hearing the concept is often a dead-end. It leads you to spending a lot of energy building friendships or chasing people in the hopes they will convert – which if you think about it is not really much of a friendship anyway. On the other hand, if someone in the world around you starts to see the light shining from your life and begins to pull on you, then spend the extra time to invest in them could change their life.

Remember, the key is always invitation, "come follow me." (Matt 4:19) When you invite someone to something, they are taking a step which activates their faith. We have relationships at some level with people we work with, people we see at places we frequent, and people we go to school with. These provide natural opportunities to invest and invite. We are inviting them to come on the journey with us, not just hanging out where they are, hoping they'll see the light.

Before John Wimber was known for the supernatural, he was known for his remarkable success in evangelism. In those days, the Vineyard was doing personal house visits to follow up on response cards. Wimber would often find himself in those visits leading someone to Jesus. When asked about it, he said that he was not remarkable at giving the gospel, just very well attuned to knowing where someone was in their journey and what they were ready for. They had already taken a step, and he knew when it was time to help them over the finish line.

I get to travel a lot with my current job role, which brings me in contact with lots of different people. Rather than put myself under pressure to share the gospel with every person I meet, I have learned to simply stay sensitive to the Holy Spirit for the opportunity of impacting them for God. In some cases, this has led to some really fun and amazing stories that only God could have scripted. In other cases, it just became moments where I could share little parts of my testimony.

Since I'm in prison ministry, people are very intrigued to know how I got into it. This opens up the door for me to tell the amazing and supernatural story of how God moved me from my previous professional employment into prison ministry. I don't tell them with the mindset to convert them, I'm just literally testifying about God's activity in my life. If they are ready, they can pull that thread and I will give them more. If they are not ready, the story will just stick with them and God can use that later. Regardless, in almost all cases, both of us are blessed. I get to celebrate what Jesus has done, and they heard a great story.

These are the stories we need to coach people to tell. Many of us were trained to tell lost people the story of our salvation, and even to think of this as the only story of what God has done in our lives. But thank God He is living and active *now,* not just yesterday. Some people have a really great story about how they were on drugs and got radically saved, but most people don't have that kind of story. The great thing is that you don't need it. You only need to know the story of what God has done and *is doing* in your life He is always active in every detail, and for many people, it's just a matter of learning to see Him in there and then sharing that.

We also need to coach people to be aware of their audience. Start by getting a sense of how open someone is before you launch in on them. Remember the Engel scale: not everyone is in the same place in their readiness to be saved or even to hear about God. I've told the same exact story about my transition into prison ministry many times, and a few times it has led to the person responding with great hunger. Most times though, it just leads to "Wow, that's really cool." And on at least one occasion, it led to rather chilly response from my seatmate. I'm certainly not going to let the chilly response from one person stop me from telling the others who are desperate to hear or open.

So, while you of course can tell a non-believer the story of your salvation, it's just as good and sometimes better, to share how God is woven into your everyday life. One time I had an Uber driver on a day literally filled with divine appointments, and he said to me, "Is your life always like this?" I had to laugh and say that while it isn't always, it does happen more than you would think! I got to pray for him and give him prophetic encouragement before I got out of the car. I would have led him in a prayer of salvation if he had been ready for it, but he wasn't quite yet. I didn't leave disappointed because I didn't "close the deal." I left overjoyed because I know this young man was deeply touched by God. Of course, telling someone who is in the "Ready" category about Jesus is downright thrilling! And you can't always tell who is in that category.

## OUTREACH TEAMS

With the right evangelistically minded people, you can take a step beyond personal outreach by having outreach teams that go out in the style of Todd White, where they approach random people for the purpose of praying for their healing or giving them words of knowledge. Kevin Dedmon has developed this into a repeatable play called the *Treasure Hunt.*

*When we reach out, the Holy Spirit is inviting us to participate in one step on someone's journey.*

We are bringing Jesus into the earth and into the lives of regular people—so we should act like the regular people that we are, not like people pushing hard to sell product. When we reach out, the Holy Spirit is inviting us to participate in one step on someone's journey. It may be the first or the last, but it's just one step. And if we have a real relationship with Jesus, we should make Him relatable, even when that involves the miraculous.

Reaching out can do wonders for the faith and culture of your church because it moves people into "mission mode," increases their faith, and blesses people. Keep in mind, though, that in the days of Amazon and limitless media, fewer and fewer people are ever even on "the streets." A street team does wonders for evangelistic culture but it's not the only way evangelism happens—or even the most common way. You want to build a church where everything that happens is evangelistic in one way or another. Personal outreach is just one component of that.

One of the surprising things about doing miracles on the streets is that, for many people, it's still just a step in their journey. We imagine that a miracle will be the irrefutable point of conversion, and for some it is. But for others even a miracle is not enough. We see this in the dialogue of one of Jesus' parables:

'No, father Abraham,' he said, 'but if someone from the dead goes to them, they will repent.' "He said to him, 'If they do not listen to Moses and the Prophets, they will not be convinced even if someone rises from the dead.' (Luke 16:30-31)

In addition, there are miracles in the Bible such as the Day of Pentecost where fire came from heaven and they all spoke in tongues, but *still* some of those present said they were just drunk (Acts 2:15).

So even when we're moving in the miraculous, the same rules apply. We're offering people an invitation to take a step forward. It may make them ready to come to Jesus, it may be the next step in their journey, or it may not have any directly noticeable effect on their faith at all. Go out and pray for people and see what God does anyway. If they become open, explain the gospel. But if they don't, you can just bless them on their way.

Additionally, if they are in the middle—and most people

actually are—then it's important that you recognize that and do follow-up. Before you go out, consider what kinds of people will you encounter, and what will you invite them to do as their next step? Put another way, if you go fishing, have a plan for what to do with the fish. At minimum you should have contact cards for your church so people can reach back if God moves them. Or even better, connect your outreach to your "inreach." Invite them to come to a church event or other personal connection point where they might be comfortable. Don't be disappointed if they don't come. Remember, it usually takes more than one step to get someone over the finish line.

Most salvations actually happen through a "chain." One person is saved and if you follow up well with that one person, then many of the other people connected to their life have the potential to be saved. Another person in that tree can lead to the process repeating itself, producing exponential growth. This is what happened to the Philippian jailer in Acts 16, as well as to the woman at the well in John 4. One door leads to another – and God knows where to knock! Therefore, don't worry so much about the 10 people who don't follow up after they are healed or prayed for, just make sure to really invest in the one who does.

The goal of all outreach and awareness tactics is simply to get someone to take their next step on their journey with God—often by coming to church where they will have a deeper and more definite encounter with Jesus. Once they are there, you want them to encounter His people in a loving and safe environment. And you want them to actually meet Jesus. This is where the Outreach System ends and the Encounter System begins.

# The Encounter Message

## ROLE OF THE SUNDAY SERVICE

If our outreach is successful it should lead to people visiting the Sunday service. The question is what will happen when they get there? In the traditional model, even though it is not always explicitly stated, the Sunday service is understood to be a gathering of believers who hear a message that is geared towards them as believers. While this is edifying to them, it speaks very little to a non-churched person. The traditional model therefore generally leads to preaching to the choir—in many cases, literally!

Of course all pastors want to see people saved which is why at the end of the message, an invitation is typically given to any non-believer who may happen to be in the service. But unless work is done to bring non-believers to the service, they won't be there to hear the truth. You end up asking your own people to be resaved over and over. On the other hand, if work is done to bring non-believers to the service, then we have to ask will the message they hear be tuned to address them where they are, or will they hear internal shop-talk that doesn't relate to them?

To address this problem, the seeker-oriented model of church tunes everything toward non-believers (seekers). The message is adjusted accordingly, toning down Christian vocabulary, reducing confrontational language, and generally focusing on being relatable to the world outside church. And to its credit, the seeker-oriented service and message can be incredibly effective at drawing large crowds. In general, if you were to plot churches in America by size, the larger the church, the more generic the message. Joel Osteen, for example, who preaches in an arena, gives breezy messages which are often devoid of the traditional gospel. Yet he has managed to gather one of the largest crowds in America *and* is followed by non-believers who find his messages encouraging.

Behind this is the seeker-driven theory that, over time, people become comfortable with going to church and Christianity in general, and then will progressively want to know more about Jesus. Somewhere along the line, they will get saved.

While the seeker-oriented service can draw large crowds, including many who would otherwise not be interested in church, all that glitters is not gold. It has some significant drawbacks. The foremost of these is the placebo effect. Intentionally making people who are not in a relationship with Jesus feel comfortable removes an important incentive to convert: if you are comfortable being a non-believer, why become a believer? Given the eternal stakes at hand, this proposition can be hazardous to people's souls.

Secondly, and almost just as importantly, is the starvation effect it produces within believers who attend. In a traditional service, you are speaking to believers or "feeding the sheep." But in the seeker model, you are speaking to non-believers and using your service to draw them in, which can starve the sheep. In the best case, everyone is drinking milk all the time. In the worst case, the gospel itself is watered down or not proclaimed.

You can't live a healthy and productive Christian life drinking milk. You have to progress to meaty things—in fact it's God will that you do (1 Corinthians 3:2)! As the leader, the words you do or don't speak over your people have power. If you talk more about TV shows than the Bible, then people are confirmed in their interest in TV rather than developing a hunger for the Bible. If you don't discuss and model a radical hunger for God, people won't have it. If you don't use passionate and intense emotion and language, then they will not develop that kind of language. Your people will become who they see you to be.

*Your people will become who they see you to be.*

Similarly, seeker services will often do

things like intentionally change terminology to sound like contemporary business language rather than church language, and temper strong Christian messages to be simply encouraging messages. If you use a lot of corporate language, people begin to feel and act "corporate" about church. Ironically, many pastors see this as a good thing since it helps professionalize what could be an overly emotional environment. Yet most people who work in the corporate world would tell you they experience daily professionalism as empty and sterile. Corporate environments are clean but impersonal. You know people there, but your real friends are elsewhere. Sterilizing terminology sterilizes the church itself.

Leaders of a seeker-oriented church may hope or assume that people will get the "meat" somewhere else, like a small group or a growth track meeting. But because the Sunday service is the only shared experience among all your congregants, it is the defining experience. The way the pastor talks on Sunday sets the standard for how the church will think and talk the rest of the week. I have never seen a significant exception to this rule. People believe what you tell them, and so if we want to produce mature disciples, it is absolutely essential that we give them mature words of life on Sunday.

## WHAT SHOULD THE MESSAGE BE?

What kind of message is appropriate for encounter-based services? The goal is to give a message which will reach those who have come far enough to be encountered for the first time, but will also inspire those have been with you for a long time. Each hearer should be brought to Jesus and led to consider their next step in that moment of their lives.

Practically speaking, you should preach from the heart more than the head. Tell personal stories that connect with people, building up to a "What does this mean for me?" moment. Then invite them to respond. Prepare your message but give yourself enough room to follow the bunny trails that the Holy Spirit might give you while you're talking. My experience is that these are almost always the Holy Spirit bringing in something powerful and specific that will change at least one person's life in your audience. They seem only partly related but are sometimes the word of knowledge that sets someone free.

I believe Jesus did this. One of the things about Jesus that was baffling to the disciples was His communication style—not just what He said, but why He said specific things to specific people.

> The disciples came to him and asked, "Why do you speak to the people in parables?" He replied, "Because the knowledge of the secrets of the kingdom of heaven has been given to you, but not to them. Whoever has will be given more, and they will have an abundance. Whoever does not have, even what they have will be taken from them. This is why I speak to them in parables." (Matthew 13:10-13)

While this may sound harsh at first pass, it's actually a very effective communication strategy. Not everyone is ready or able to receive the full revelation that Jesus wants to give. Everyone has different educational background and life experience, and are in different places in their walk with God. Parables allow more touchpoints. The disciples themselves were not ready to receive the full revelation Jesus had, especially when they first got going. Near the end of Jesus ministry, though, He began to speak to them more directly:

> Then Jesus' disciples said, "Now you are speaking clearly and without figures of speech. Now we can see that you know all things and that you do not even need to have anyone ask you questions. This makes us believe that you came from God." (John 16:29-30)

On their end, the disciples probably thought Jesus was being cagey by speaking in parables, but actually He was opening their hearts to take them on a journey of truth. He was picking them up from wherever they were, which was different for each of them. Only after several years of walking with Him were they all together, on the same page, and ready for the full revelation. The parables and figures of speech were their gateway into deeper revelation. As they reflected on and accepted those teaching, they moved closer to Jesus.

This is why Jesus says that "those who have will be given more" (Luke 19:26). If you have some revelation and you respond to it, it will open up the door for God to reveal more. However, if you do not steward the revelation you have, then you will move away from God and toward darkness. This is why He is always saying, "He who has ears to hear, let him hear." He's inviting and challenging people to respond and come closer.

This is an important Scriptural insight, and one that we need to be careful to apply correctly. The recognition that Jesus did not give the fullness of truth to everyone has led some growth-oriented churches to adjust their language and terminology on Sunday so much that it would be hard for a believer to recognize the service as church! I visited a very large church with this theory a number of years ago. The pastor got an exercise ball, talked about "building your core," and told people that Jesus was the way that he himself chose to build his core, but they might have other ways.

While I know he was doing this as an evangelistic technique, what I have experienced with this approach over time is that the same cues which tell non-believers that they belong cause them to stay where they are and not become committed believers. The preacher with the exercise ball was communicating in a way that I might communicate when dealing with an "uncontacted" group – people out in the world that have not made any choice to seek him, like Paul did on Mars Hill. It's also the way that I might speak if given a large public platform in a secular setting – using their language and worldview to generate interest in Jesus. It's a valid way to communicate, but it presumes encounter is going to happen somewhere else. In the encounter-based church, we are speaking the truth in the power of the Spirit with the intention that God is going to encounter people here.

On the other end of the spectrum, the unfiltered approach can be equally damaging. My wife and I brought some non-believing family members to church for Easter many years ago, and our pastor chose that Sunday to preach on a very contentious political topic. It had a devastating effect on our attempts to reach them for Christ. My family missed their encounter because they got scared away. They ended up seeing our church as a kind of fringe political group rather than a place where they could meet God. If our pastor had had more attunement to the audience and the purpose of the Sunday message, things could have been quite different.

In both cases above, the preaching and service failed the test of encounter. The first was because you would be hard pressed to find Jesus, and the second was because the message was so strong, that you'd be likely to run from Him. The low-bar message about the exercising your core did not have any application that brought people to Jesus. There was no motive, setting, or expectation for encounter. And the hardcore message my visiting family heard was "inside baseball" for very committed members and disciples, not everyone at large—especially in a context like Easter where there was a high probability that non-believers would be present.

*The question you have to ask is, "Does my message pass the encounter test?"* In the encounter-based church model, the question you have to ask is, "Does my message pass the encounter test?" It should be tuned in such a way that it will invite both those who have never met Jesus and those who know Him to be encountered by Him. Thinking about the Engel Scale, and who we expect to be in a Sunday meeting gives us framework for how to apply this concept. Let's look at some different demographics present in our audience.

You want the Sunday message to speak to any "unconverted"

who have been brought, who have come far enough to be present. You also want to speak to your friends and believers who are present all of the time. We want to preach in such a way that they are invited into a deeper walk with Him from wherever they are. Hitting this note in the Sunday service ensures that people can come on the journey and will find more than just the basics of life (milk) but not too much inside baseball.

| Group | Messages Must |
|---|---|
| Uncontacted | Relate to their world |
| **Unconverted** | **Invite to our world** |
| **Believer** | **Inspire and challenge** |
| Member | Instruct and train |
| Disciple | Make them effective |
| Leader | Show them where to have impact. |

### GETTING THE CONTENT

When you a preaching for encounter, it is very important to preach into what God is doing in your congregation at that time. Unfortunately, most mainstream preaching resources teach you to do exactly the opposite: to preach from a text for predefined concept. As a Spirit-filled believer, you have the great luxury of starting by asking God for what He wants to communicate and plant into your church or the Body at large at this time.

Once you have a sense of where God wants to go, then ask Him for the Scriptures that relate to that topic, as well as personal stories or cultural references which will illustrate that point in a way that people remember. People rarely remember abstract content, but a great story they will never forget.

As you do this, consider where most people in your congregation are going to be, and how to bridge that. In a medium to large congregation there will be many people with serious life issues going on – life threatening or undiagnosable illness, loss or potential loss of close family members, job or financial trouble, and serious marital or divorce-related challenges are some of the most common. In addition, every week there are people who the enemy has been working hard to discourage, or who want to know how to be better parents, Christians, or decision-makers.

If you want to create encounter, make sure to speak to people in the midst of where they really are. Part of what made Jesus so compelling was that he was able to relate to sinners, tax collectors, lepers and divorcees from exactly where they were. Sometimes the business of the life of a leader can make you feel insulated from what is going on during the week with your congregation or the world around you. If this is you, it may help to solicit information through your associate, secretary, or someone else active in the care network. Being able to have a face in mind as you form your message is invaluable for hitting home, and will usually strike a chord with more than just the individual you are thinking of.

Getting enough content for inspiring messages can exhaust even extraordinarily gifted pastors. That is why it is wise to split your messages into series. You will likely burn yourself out preparing disconnected messages every week because of the amount of spiritual energy and intellectual preparation it takes.

Preaching a series allows you time to adequately develop a theme, and also makes preparation much easier. It also takes time-pressure off the delivery of the message. When you're trying to cram a real revelation into a single message, it's easy to hit 45-60 minutes. Unfortunately, in a world where a 10-minute YouTube clip of highly unique content is considered long, a 60-minute message might as well be considered an eternity. Your goal for the message should be 30-40 minutes, driving toward one powerful application point where you invite response and give an opportunity for the Holy Spirit to move. If people take away one life-changing point, you've done a great service for a Sunday.

Remember the old preacher's adage that "the man is the message." Some preachers put so much emphasis on preparation of the content that they neglect the preparation of their person. When I preach, I pray to get the message and I do the work to assemble it, but once I have it, the most important part is to bring the atmosphere of the Holy Spirit with me. On the day of the message, I never make changes, I simply pray and trust the Holy Spirit to move through me.

*When people connect emotionally with a speaker, they give permission in their hearts for the truth to go in.*

When you deliver your messages, leave yourself room to follow the Spirit. If you feel prompted to tell a story that was not in your notes, it is often exactly the story that someone in that service needs to hear. It's more important that you be vulnerable and relatable than it is that you be impressive. When people connect emotionally with a speaker, they give permission in their hearts for the truth to go in. When they laugh and cry with you, they will come on the journey with you. Assemble those pieces to drive home to a point, and then pray so that this point comes to life through you. For more coaching on the fundamentals of assembling a message, you might consider *Communicating for a Change* by Andy Stanley. While Stanley does not write from an explicitly Spirit-filled perspective, I think he does a good job as simplifying into understandable terms the process of making a message that will actually connect with your hearers.

Along with this, I think we can be convicting without being condemning. If we avoid challenging people on the difficult topics of faith, we're depriving them of the opportunity to grow and continue their journey toward Jesus. On the other hand, if we preach hard jeremiads, the net impression that people will leave with is that God is difficult and harsh. God the Father and God the Son loved us to the point of death (John 3:16), so if our preaching doesn't leave the impression of that depth of love, we're doing something wrong.

We should have and give off more joy than anyone in the world ever could. Remember, we love because He first loved us (1 John 4:19). When people see that and know that, they will want not only to come back to service, but they will want to know God in that way. If this strikes a chord with you, you might want to read my book *No Exit*, where I explore this in more detail and discuss my exodus from unfeeling religion into warm relationship with Jesus.

## KEEPING THE MESSAGE BROAD

Remember that the Sunday service is people's place of encounter. The harder you push sectarian doctrines, the smaller you limit your community. Now, do hear me on this: I'm not suggesting that you boil everything doctrinal out to the point where the content has no teeth. But I am challenging the idea that the Sunday service is the appropriate place to ride niche doctrines.

Jesus actually rebuked the teachers of His day for their over-attention to secondary doctrines.

> Woe to you, scribes and Pharisees, hypocrites! For you tithe mint and dill and cumin, and have neglected the weightier matters of the law: justice and mercy and faithfulness. These you ought to have done, without neglecting the others. (Matthew 23:23)

By focusing on the letter of the Law, the Pharisees created an environment that was unbalanced. According to Jesus, in order create a healthy environment people need to be fed on the "weightier matters" like the mercy and faithfulness of God. This means we avoid rabbit trails that we love to go down because of our background or pet interests. The "second trumpet blast in Revelation" or "the inner chambers of the portals of heaven" may be interesting to you personally but is not generally edifying for the body at large.

Remember who is there, and what the function of the service is. You want people to encounter Jesus in the power of the Holy Spirit and go further with Him. You might have some things which are very important to you but are not the most appropriate for the public Sunday service. They may in fact push people away from you, church, or God. Niche topics are sometimes fascinating but better for those who voluntarily choose to go deeper with you as disciples. As you gain trust and people become more involved in the community, they are more likely to move toward your beliefs on many other topics.

*Before you preach, ask your yourself, "How does this practically matter in the lives of my listeners?"*

This non-sectarian approach has the effect of making room for a wider spectrum of people to be present and enjoy fellowship with you. Before you preach, ask your yourself, "How does this practically matter in the lives of my listeners?" If you can't answer that question clearly, then move to something more directly applicable. Our church places a very high degree of focus on building relationship with Jesus. It's the main theme of most sermons. I found this to be a great relief because, looking back on my Christian life, most churches I have attended have made something else the main message. Yet relationship with Jesus is worthy to be the focus of our faith!

This approach has another healthy side effect: it diminishes a frequent cause of intra-church conflict. By putting core doctrines that everyone should believe at the center—such as relationship with Jesus, or the authority of Scripture, encounter with the Holy Spirit, honoring the Father, etc.—and by keeping obscure or contentious points at the edge, this keeps the dialogue where you want to have it. If you are going to have a conflict in your church, you want it to be about something that is truly core to your identity and nonnegotiable for a follower of Christ.

# The Encounter Service

## TUNING THE SERVICE

To review, the idea of the encounter-based church is to create a space where 1) someone who has made the journey to be open to encountering Jesus for the first time is likely to encounter Him, and 2) those who need a fresh encounter with Him will also be touched. While this may sound contradictory to those who have been either building a seeker-based expression or a full Charismatic expression, my experience is that the two are not in contradiction.

That's the beauty of the person of Jesus – when He shows up, He touches everyone exactly where they are. When I have had the pleasure of being in a service where the Spirit is strongly present, I am always amazed at how many different ways people can be touched through the same message. The words that came out in English were the same, but the Living Word that was heard was calibrated by His presence.

*Our job is to simply create an environment where He can do what only He can do.*

Our job is to simply create an environment where He can do what only He can do. This means reviewing all aspects of the service with that in mind. If we were to tune your service with the specific goal of welcoming Jesus, what would it look like? I think of this a little bit like planning a great date. If my wife and I just go out to eat, we'll have a nice time. But if I want her to have a really special time, I need to give some thought to all of the components of the experience: how I treat her, how we get there, planning the childcare, the atmosphere, the food, and what we do afterwards. None of these components by themselves is going to create a deep intimate moment, but they set the table by communicating value to her, and giving her the mental space, the emotional space, and the setting where she is comfortable opening her heart.

My experience with the moving of the Spirit in a corporate setting is similar. When applied properly, structure facilitates the work of the Holy Spirit, it doesn't constrict it. It becomes the altar on which we can place the fire. But this means we must build the structure to intentionally invite and welcome Him. Otherwise our finely tuned altar will be empty.

In an *attractional model*, tight scripting of the service is the rule of the day. There is an exact number of songs of a very specific length, with an exact sermon length, and announcements or other video of a very specific length, sometimes down to the second. If there are multiple campuses, the sequence in each is timed to correlate exactly. A structure this tight really cramps the ability for the Spirit to encounter people. Keeping with the analogy of a great date, how would the date go if you planned things so tightly that your wife didn't have room to express her feelings and tell you what was on her mind? I would suggest you probably missed the entire point of the date! All of the work you do in planning is to create an atmosphere where she can connect to you, feel heard, and feel loved. An exact script won't work.

On the other hand, when we talk about creating a service where the Holy Spirit can move, it usually conjures up pictures of the most ungoverned kinds of behavior that could be observed in a Charismatic service – people randomly shouting out, ruining the moment, or interrupting the service. Or it creates the idea that there will be no plan at all – that we are more spiritual if we announce that the Holy Spirit just changed our plans and we're going to do something completely different than we were expecting to do.

While God can definitely surprise us, it's not the norm. If you're living a life of communion with Jesus, then the normal way for God to work is through your plans, not in spite of them. This is because He has been speaking to you through the week, not just surprising you at the last second.

What are we talking about then, when we say that we are making room for the Spirit to move? It means that we want God to encounter people in the corporate service, so we provide different opportunities for that to happen in a way that blesses the corporate body. And if we sense that God is working in a special way, then we don't pass by it – just like if your wife starts to open up and share her heart with you on the date, then everything stops and you go with it!

**Worship.** The first and most obvious application of this is in the worship part of the service. Worship is the time when the Lord encounters us in ways that surpass words. People drop their burdens and are touched by the Lord. Does your worship leader have the freedom to give Spirit-led encouragements during the set? Can they repeat or extend a song that seems to be really working? Does the team know how to move out into a prophetic moment if they feel led to do so, to pray for healing for example? Then if the Spirit starts to work in a special way, are you prepared to jump in and steward that? Do you have the flexibility to enter into a time of waiting on the Lord in a holy hush? If not at the beginning of a service, how about at the end?

When your script is too tight, you will miss these kinds of moments, or worse, try to prevent them to keep everything on track. Like every form of art, we have to make room for the human element. In doing so, I believe we make room for Jesus, who Himself took on the form of a man.

The style of your praise and worship is also important. If you are in a traditional church, then of course nothing is a more sensitive topic than the music style. I do not think that there is only one musical style God can encounter people with, but I also observe that the global church goes through seasons where a particular style is more effective than another, probably due to cultural expectations. Therefore, I believe that tracking with the music that is fresh in the "now" in your community is an important part to having encounter. We should "move with the cloud," as they say.

With this in mind, worship is not just the *what* or the *how*, it's the *who*. If you want a powerful encounter-based meeting, you need a team that has consecrated themselves as worshippers. At minimum this includes leading a lifestyle of purity – it's better to be missing a part of the band than to have someone on the team living in sin. Is your team large enough and equipped enough to allow those in struggling seasons to take a break?

It also includes leading a lifestyle of worship personally. Great worship leaders and team members are constantly renewing their connection with Jesus through their own worship. Cultivating this atmosphere on the team is one of the primary goals of the worship leader. In addition, the team needs to rehearse and pray. Without sufficient practice the music will not be quality, and without prayer, it will not be anointed.

At bare minimum, the team should pray together before every service with enough time for each person to engage in the prayer or be prayed over. The benefit of outside meetings where the team can gel and connect with each other, working out kinks, developing their skills, composing, praying, etc., should not be overlooked. Heart-level connection with each other and with the congregation will make all the difference in what happens when the music starts.

**Prayer Moments.** Similarly, think about the moments of prayer you have in your service. Is it token prayer, only at the very beginning or the very end? Do you only pray over the congregation, or do you pray *with* the congregation? Is it ten seconds, or do you have time to linger a few minutes? These are the kinds of things that make a super tight service schedule very constricting, but when you loosen them, the Spirit can move.

Make sure you make it participatory. The service is not a

show. Invite people to engage the prayer by stretching their hands forward or putting their hand on their heart. If you want them to pray for marriages or children, consider asking them to lay hands on their own family members next to them. Connect with God yourself before you start, even if it just takes an extra thirty seconds. If you want your service to be enjoyable and full of life, it's very important that you not be the only person on the platform. Leverage the talent that is hidden within your congregation and create opportunities for leaders.

In addition, if you have not practiced praying prayers of adoration and praise, you should. The Psalms give us a model of what this kind of prayer looks like. Take a look at this little passage from Psalm 145:1-2 (Passion).

> My heart explodes with praise to you!
> Now and forever my heart bows in worship to you,
> my King and my God!
> Every day I will lift up my praise to your name
> with praises that will last throughout eternity.

The Psalmist begins the Psalm by telling God how amazing He is. As we lift God up, it takes our eyes off our ourselves and puts our eyes onto Him. Life through the week puts our minds onto earthly things and our own weaknesses, but when we come into worship and fix our eyes on Him, it puts us into a completely different frame of mind – one that is ready for encounter.

**Testimony** is a critical part of an encounter-based service, but is often left out. If God is working in your church, then one certain way to see that more is to spotlight those who are being touched and let them tell their story. This creates a viral effect where the faith of others is stirred to believe for the same thing in their life.

All pastors know there is risk involved in bringing another person up to share their story. But in my view, that risk is worth

*When services become hyper-produced they lose the human element, yet it is the human element that God works through to touch others.* the reward. When services become hyper-produced they lose the human element, yet it is the human element that God works through to touch others. I am not suggesting that you have open mic. This leads to random people sharing "testimonies" that quench the Spirit. Instead create a process where your leaders can report to you the stories of what God is doing in the Body during the week:, significant things like physical healings, relationships being restored, bondages being broken, past wounds being healed. Choose some trusted ones to highlight or coach the person to summarize their story well. Or if time is an issue, bring them up on stage with you and summarize it for them but honor Jesus with a real moment of praise! Seek these testimonies during the week. They never get old because they remind us that Jesus is alive.

**Message.** We discussed the approach and content of the message in the last chapter, but in terms of the flow of the encounter service, remember that the function of the message is to lead people from where they are toward an encounter with Jesus. We want to show what Jesus is like. We are preaching or teaching toward a better walk with Him, not just informing. We can use other venues in our growth system to teach more thoroughly, but on Sunday we want to challenge, inspire, and invite people to encounter the living God throughout their week. Don't be afraid to break the flow and engage the congregation directly. If the congregation feels distant from you, they will feel distant from God too.

**Invitation.** The normal conclusion of a service should be an invitation that is specific to the message that was preached. It should also include an invitation to meet Jesus for the first time, and a general offer for prayer. You don't want to give the same high-pressure emotional appeal every week, as this can have the effect of dampening the power of the appeal over time. But you should have a genuine opportunity for Spirit-led response as is appropriate for the message and moment.

For example, if your message is on being sensitive to God's voice and His leading, then make the general offer for prayer something around that subject, like wanting to hear God better, or forgiveness if you think you've been resisting Him. You can pray something like, "If you're saying right now, God I've been running from your voice..." As you step out in faith this way, you may find that you are actually stepping into a Spirit-led amplification of thoughts that many people are thinking. During the invitation, music normally plays in the background to create an atmosphere of openness.

**Altar Time.** Trained altar workers should be down front to pray and minister to people in a way that brings them to Jesus. Many Spirit-filled workers are trained to first ask if someone knows Jesus, and then to ask if they are filled with the Holy Spirit. While there is definitely some merit to that approach, my experience is that in a time of response the altar team should be focused to what Jesus is doing in that person in relation to the message which brought them there.

I'll never forget when our pastor preached on forgiveness and a young woman practically ran down and burst out sobbing. She was convicted of her need to forgive. It was not the moment to run her through the checklist, but a time to partner with what Jesus was doing in her life. We spent a couple of hours helping her through the process, and it ended up being a key turning point on her journey.

The altar should be "safe space" where hearers can respond to what's going on in their hearts, which is where God is working. They can unload their burdens and receive a touch from heaven instead. For this reason, we make an effort to be sensitive to where people are in their walk with the Lord, and not do things like pray loudly in tongues over people who may not be familiar with the Holy Spirit. That can be done in a subsequent step if needed, or in a private area.

During our altar time, which normally lasts about 10-15 minutes but can be extended afterwards in an adjoining area if needed, we use the ALMA model: **A**sk, **L**isten, **M**inister, **A**ctivate. We ask questions and listen carefully to people as well as to the Holy Spirit to try to understand where the person is and what prayer needs to be prayed at that time. Then we minister through prayer, inviting the Holy Spirit to touch them. Finally we try to identify an activation step to follow-up. This may be as simple as inviting them to come back again but sometimes involves introducing them to someone else, or recommending another ministry step in the church. My book, *School of the Spirit,* is a complete training course for Spirit-filled altar workers.

**Total Duration.** Sometimes in a Spirit-filled setting, we can pride ourselves on the sermon going over or having a long service. If genuine move of God breaks out with people running to the altar, or a glory cloud appears in the meeting, or people start getting out of wheelchairs, by all means, I fully believe you should go absolutely as long as God is working! On the other hand, in most normal scenarios, we will do better by placing a high value on people's time and attention.

The longer a service is, the more engaging components it needs to have in order to work. As a point of reference, keep in mind that the average Hollywood film, which hundreds of people work on for months or years to make incredibly engaging, is around 90 minutes. In a normal scenario, I would suggest that you set that as the absolute cap for your total service length, and better if you can do it in less.

Put all together, the pieces of your Sunday service are designed to cultivate an atmosphere of corporate encounter, and to bless both individuals and the larger Body. We should not underestimate the power of a corporate encounter. When you actively partner with Jesus throughout the service to encourage the ministry moments, from the worship all the way through to the altar, a great deal of ministry can be accomplished that might otherwise take a lot of time and energy to address in other settings.

## WHEN GOD MOVES

If you are doing a good job setting the table for God to come then many weeks he is going to move in small but significant ways – people will come forward crying, people will be healed or set free during the worship, people will hear Him speaking to them during your message. This is what a "normal" service will look like when you're doing it right. Every once in a while, however, God may do something special, that is beyond the norm.

When He does, you should be ready to go with it, for exactly that reason – after much preparation, the Guest of Honor has appeared. Thinking again about the analogy of a date, I always look forward to having a great date with my wife, but every once in a while, we have a really special moment of breakthrough. If that happens, all bets are off. I don't drive home, I stop and tune into her because nothing else matters. I'm not going to miss my moment of visitation. If He shows up, are you ready to extend or redirect the service? Or simply make room for the unexpected?

What makes this challenging when talking about spiritual matters, however is that when Jesus shows up in a significant way, the human response can be all over the map. In the early days of the Vineyard, John Wimber, he invited the powerful but controversial evangelist Lonnie Frisbee to help him with the meeting on Mother's Day, 1980. Everything was going well until at the end of the meeting Lonnie grabbed the mic and said "Come Holy Spirit!" At that point, the Holy Spirit hit the congregation and the otherwise average congregation were suddenly all over the floor on top of each other.

No one could have predicted this or even coached it, and it was quite messy. Jesus showed up and did something special, and the Vineyard, a movement that changed the global church, was born. Wimber could have played it safe by not inviting Frisbee, or He could have tried to shut down the moving of the Spirit when it happened, but his choice to welcome God at a greater level opened the door to much greater things.

Of course, as leaders we know that this takes great courage and certainly Wimber got a lot of heat behind the scenes, and so one factor to face is simply being willing to "go there" with God. But the other factor, equally important, bur rarely discussed is the tendency of Spirit-filled people to "fake it till you make it." If you've been in, or heard about a service where the Spirit moved powerfully, then you want to experience it again. But this quickly leads to a culture of people trying to make it happen when in reality very little is happening, and I believe, in fact an atmosphere where it hard to host a deeper move of the Spirit, because someone is always quenching it with their fleshly behavior.

Perhaps the most common thing in this category is the so called "courtesy drop." When the Spirit moves powerfully it is common for one or many people to be knocked off of their feet. This is logical, Biblical (Rev 1:17) and historical.[3] However, this can create a culture where people are expected to fall over or even pushed over to prove that God is moving. This is why many contemporary ministers have simply said "no catchers." If you go down, it better be the Spirit, because no one will be there to catch you. I could cite many other such behaviors where "what began in the Spirit" has "ended in the flesh." (Gal 3:3). These are exactly the kinds of things we want to avoid if we expect our church to be a place that grows and non-believers are reached.

Therefore, if you want to have a true encounter-based church you have to be willing to host Jesus when he comes in a special way, but you also have to resist the culture that tries to gin something up that isn't really happening. Failing to do

---

[3] See accounts of the Cane Ridge Revival for a prominent historical example.

so not only prevents these powerful moments, it also has the side effect of ignoring the miracles Jesus is doing in your congregation during normal weeks. Not every date with my wife is a trip to the Louvre, sometimes we talk about life and eat Mexican food.

## THE HUMAN ENCOUNTER

Now we turn to figuring out how each person who attends your service will have a great experience that will lead to them being touched by God. Thinking again about the how a sales funnel works, a great deal of effort must be expended to get one lead to show interest. For a point of reference, the clickthrough ratio on an ad that is placed on a Google search is a little less than 2%. In other words, 50X more people have awareness than have actually taken action. This means that everyone visiting your church for the first time is highly valuable – the result of all of the work you did upstream to get them there. You want to make sure that they have the best experience possible.

The first part of capitalizing on that lead is everything we've already discussed—crafting the message, creating an environment that is as conducive as possible for God to encounter them on a Sunday. One powerful encounter with the Holy Spirit can change a life in a way nothing else can.

*We usually encounter Jesus through His Body before we encounter Him personally.*

At the same time, not everyone is going to have a God-encounter the very first time. It takes time for God to bring someone to readiness. This means that the other encounter that they need in your church is the *human* encounter. We usually encounter Jesus through His Body before we encounter Him personally.

For these reasons, it's important that we think about and ensure that each guest at your service has an awesome and connecting experience from a human perspective as well from a God perspective. The corporate church must help people across the bridge from feeling like outsiders – which everyone does their first few times – to feeling like insiders. From a sociological perspective, religious conversion occurs when the strength of your connections to a new group becomes greater than the strength of your connections to your old group. People have lots of old groups—friends, family, coworkers, neighbors, that all influence them. It can be a hard process. Try and make it as easy as possible.

Remember, all social groups naturally turn inwards unless they are continually encouraged to be inclusive. This is why inclusion starts at the door. Figure out who the most welcoming people in your congregation are and ask them to become the greeters at the door of your church. Their warmth and inclusive personalities will do miracles by itself. If your church has a secretary, info booth, or other central place where guests and new members go, make sure you put a warm and patient person there too!

> *People stay at a church where they feel some level of connection to the senior leader.*

In addition, if you are the pastor, your personal presence is incredibly important. It can't be overestimated that people stay at a church where they feel some level of connection to the senior leader. Before and after service are essential times for you to work the room and greet people. Guests are usually very easy to spot even in a large church, because they will just be sitting there by themselves before the start of service. Make sure your leadership team understands that this is what you'll be doing before and after service, and that you would like their help as well. Otherwise, there is a tendency for you and your leaders to spend this valuable time talking to each other instead of the high value guests that have come to meet you. Even when you are doing your best to greet, your closer friends and colleagues will come to ask you questions, chat, or comment, so you need a plan to field those well in order to target your visitors.

Consider a formal way of welcoming guests after the service, such as an invite to a side room where you meet and greet them personally. Make a space for this for a few minutes even if another leader has to close the meeting. You'll be surprised how many newcomers will feel connected to your church just because they met you.

In addition to the personal greeting, the general elements of hospitality matter. Think about the kinds of things that you or you would do if you had guests at your house. You'd make things look warm, clean, and presentable. You'd probably offer them coffee and snacks. You might even have flowers or other trimmings to warm up the room. Someone in your congregation likely has a gift of hospitality. Engage them to think about or lead in making the environment as welcoming as possible. This doesn't have to cost a fortune. A little intentionality will do it.

You should collect their information here somehow, with a "connection card" or a digital tool. If you didn't get someone's information personally, sometimes the person who brought them has it. Obviously, you need to be judicious about that, but the key here is that you make every effort to create the possibility of follow-up.

By the same token, don't leave people wondering what their next step is, or make them jump through hoops. Even if you can't get their information, it should be easy for them to reach out to you and they'll give it to you. There is no reason to hide your email on the website. Make it prominent and have someone screen for you. Let the people who want to connect do so. It worked very well for Jesus. The disciples wanted to turn the Canaanite woman away, but Jesus made it into a miracle (Matt 15:22).

Finally, follow-up is essential. In the old days people used to like a personal visit from the pastor whenever they visited the church. This is in fact how my parents decided to join the church I was raised in—the pastor made it a point to make ministry calls on people. Now our society has changed somewhat in that most people do not seem to appreciate a house call. They do still appreciate personal follow-up, however. Your follow-up could be via email, via text or if you want a really personal touch, use a handwritten card. After 5 years of going to Starbucks, I confess I still feel a bit uncomfortable there but one of the baristas happened to hand write us a Christmas card this year—asking the Lord to bless us! To be honest, I feel much more at home there now.

In addition to this personal follow-up, you should have an automated content stream which you can include visitors on. At minimum this means creating a "welcome series" with several emails that are introductory and inviting in nature. That way the person has several opportunities to engage with you if they want to. If they engage further, they should be included on a weekly newsletter which keeps people informed of what is going on.

Last, but definitely not least, I encourage you to pray over the names on the connection cards during the weekly prayer meeting the same way you pray over the prayer requests. I can never forget the dramatic story of my friend who visited a church in Australia where they asked everyone to put the names of their lost loved ones into a bucket and then prayed over them for a year. Our friend put in the name of her aunt, who was very secular and far from God. About a year later she visited the same church again and at the end of her message thought "I really wish my aunt were here to hear this." Just as she prayed this prayer, her aunt tapped her on the shoulder. Her high flying job had brought her to that same city and she wanted to surprise our friend – she heard the message and got saved! Prayer can catalyze the kinds of jaw-dropping events that no one could predict.

## HOW IT LOOKS

After the style of music, there is almost nothing more

polarizing or more revealing of your theory of church than how you look. For some, even the idea of putting energy into how things look is heretical, while for others it would seem that looks are all that mater.

Both of these mindsets contain a fundamental mistake. Remember what the Lord said to Samuel:

> People judge by outward appearance, but the LORD looks at the heart. (1 Sam. 16:7 NLT)

Whether we like it or not, this says people are going to judge us by how things look and the way we act. At the same time, if we become obsessed with how things look, we will neglect the weightier matters of the heart and become an empty vessel without substance.

This has huge consequences for how we do church, and I've seen how both play out. It's easy to become obsessed with what people think, or might think, and head down the road of assuming growth issues are solved by making minor improvements in aesthetics. Your thought processes and staff meetings become dominated with the way things appear rather than how much life and vitality the people in the congregation are receiving. At the extreme end, I fear this can make us guilty of Matthew 23:23-

> "Woe to you, scribes and Pharisees, hypocrites! For you tithe mint and dill and cumin, and **have neglected the weightier matters** of the law: justice and mercy and faithfulness. These you ought to have done, **without** neglecting the others. (Matt. 23:23 ESV)

The Pharisees were experts at doing what others would see, but did them as an empty system without heart transformation. Note carefully though, that Jesus does not say to only do the one, but He says to do both.

I believe Jesus is saying we need a balance with the scale tipped towards the "weightier matters." One on hand, we can end up focusing on the things that people see rather than the more important things they cannot see. On the other hand, a great number of well-meaning leaders believe that people will simply stream through the door simply because they are preaching well and hosting the Spirit.

We need a "both/and" approach to this problem. We need a tasty orange inside an appealing peel. If the peel looks good but the orange inside is not, then they will bite, but probably only once. If the peel doesn't look good, then no matter how tasty it is, they are unlikely to ever know how sweet the fruit is. Unfortunately, it is fairly rare to see the two practiced well together because these are competing mindsets. People tend to focus on one at the expense of the other, for reasons that are deep in the heart.

How you appear to others is a crucial part of reaching people. Perhaps one of the most important Scriptures related to evangelism is Paul's statement in 1 Corinthians 9:22 that "I have become all things to all men, so that I might by all means save some." Paul adjusted his presentation and approach to reach his target audience, and this was not just theoretical flourish. We see him speaking philosophy to the Greeks on Mars Hill in Acts 17. Then one chapter later, he shaves his head to conform to Jewish custom, even though he was against "Judaizing" the church. Paul adjusted both his message and his appearance to connect with his audience.

Howard Schultz, the CEO who made Starbucks one of the most powerful brands in the world, had the saying that "Branding is easy: everything matters." In other words, take a look at the entire experience of a new person coming in your doors, and evaluate whether it reinforces or detracts from the experience and perception you want them to have. Some factors are more obvious than others. I have listed several elements to consider below, but keep in mind that all of my comments should be contextualized for the type of church you are and who your target audience is. I would apply these very differently to a 100-year old Presbyterian church than I would to a new church plant in the urban core.

**Facility.** Is the facility inviting or foreboding? If you were an average person, would you want to come in? This starts at the curb, the sign, and the entryway. These are important because they are what everyone sees the most. Of course you may not have direct control over all of these factors, but change starts with awareness. As we described in detail in Chapter 4, give some thought to how things look, then identify steps to getting them where you want them to be. Also consider your labeling in the entryway—do new people know where to go once they are inside? Are the sanctuary, kids area, and bathrooms discoverable? It's hard for a confused visitor to feel comfortable.

If you are in a position to be considering a new facility, think about it from the angle of how natural it would be to visit. Retail spaces can be a great option. You are taking a place that people are used to going and turning it into a place where you want them to go. Of course, traditional church buildings have value as well – they will appeal to those who grew up in church but have not been in a long time (sometimes called the "de-churched"), which in our society is now quite a large segment.

Once you are inside the facility, ask yourself the same kinds of questions. Does this look like a clean, inviting and professional space, or does it look like grandma's attic? Do you have pews or chairs? If you have a choice, chairs are less formal, more comfortable, and more conducive to community. Is the carpet from the 70s? Do you have exposed wires everywhere? What about your restrooms? A bad restroom experience can leave an impression that is hard to forget. I don't mean remodeling. Just adding some new hand soap, a plastic plant, and a Christian décor sign can be enough to make your visitor feel warm and welcome.

Similarly look at your nursery area. Parents will feel better if they are dropping their children off in a place that looks secure, clean, and up to date. Again, I don't mean you need to spend a fortune. Just look at icons like a newer, functioning baby gate and swing; rooms that are painted and have something edifying on the walls. New parents will appreciate things like clearly labeled signs for who goes where, with some kind of sign in and security person. If your facility is older and can't be updated much, then even a desk out front of the child's area with some décor and a greeter is great. The point is a clean, prepped appearance of the kids' section makes a great first impression that is almost as important as the entryway.

**Platform.** Then consider the stage or platform and everything pertaining to it Is it cluttered, or open and inviting? How is the sound? Do you have frequent technical issues? Is the balance among your musicians appropriate? Is the sound too loud? Are the drums too loud? Being a little too soft will not make someone leave the church, but being a little too loud will. It's better to err on the side of a little quieter.

How do your musicians look? Today the common principle is to look coordinated and well-groomed, but with the freedom to look like the creative artists that they are. Take a look at any team from a successful church such as Hillsong to get an idea of what I mean. Of course there should be flexibility here to suit your nature and audience, but remember that people will be looking at them for as much as half of your service so they form an important part of the impression people will have about you.

Similarly, how do you and your staff look? If you are dressed up too much, you communicate distance, but if you just wear whatever you feel like in the morning, you will not project the image of someone who should be followed. Many contemporary pastors of large churches today look a bit hip— skinny jeans, great hair, and carefully chosen shoes. The jeans and blazer look is also still popular among some. But these are just possible looks. The question you need to ask is: Would my target audience follow a person dressed like I'm dressed?

Whatever your style is, put some energy into and pull it off well. The great thing about this is that you don't have to become a fashion nerd to do this. Just find a person in your congregation who is and solicit their input! They get a job which makes them a co-owner, and you get to stay focused on the things that matter most.

Once you get a sense of how you want to look, expect the same of others that you're putting in front of the congregation as leaders. Don't make it a religious axiom that "we dress this way to look good for God" because that adds a lot of baggage which can create factions. Instead, just emphasize that as leaders, you want them to project a **positive, professional image**. You want them to be role models. Your team looking good sends a good message to everyone else, and it also communicates those hidden aspects of what it means to be a leader.

The most common pitfall of becoming aware of how things look and addressing them is to become obsessed with appearances, which is a worldly pursuit. Once you start noticing things, it can open up a Pandora's box where form replaces the power and presence of the Holy Spirit. It's incredibly important to practice the 80/20 rule of allowing good enough to be good enough. Otherwise you will find yourself straining at gnats and exhausting yourself and your staff with things like why there weren't enough refreshments that morning. If taken far enough, this can escalate to the level where people feel like your faith in people being changed is actually in the brand of coffee and the number of donuts served.

This kind of thinking will literally siphon the working of the Spirit away from you. This is especially true because of the special pressure that senior leaders feel. Even before I understood the value of good presentation, I remember in our church being obsessed with the music being too loud or too soft, and it would frequent distract me the worship time that I needed to be ready to give a good message. Honestly, I doubt anyone else noticed but me.

*If something isn't perfect but it's good enough, let it not be perfect.*

The balance to considering looks and appearances is that it will always need to stay in place behind the two great commandments of loving God and loving each other. You want to do the superficial things well while still keeping them in the background. This means if something isn't perfect but it's good enough, let it not be perfect. It's more important that your team be focused on Jesus and caring about the people that come through the door than it is that you never run out of donuts.

What has to stay in the foreground is the human and relational parts of what it means to be a church. The peel is not what makes the orange tasty. When people feel and are authentically loved and celebrated, and given opportunities to minister to others, they will feel fulfilled and at home. Remember, you did a lot of work to generate the lead, and then bring that person to your church, and help them make the transition to a committed part of your body. This leads to the next step in the church funnel: The Growth System.

# Deeper Encounters

## GOING BEYOND SUNDAY

In the encounter-based church, we tune Sunday to be a space where non-believers and believers alike can be transformed by encountering Jesus. Unlike a seeker-service which is tuned exclusively to non-believers, or a traditional service which presumes everyone is already a believer, we are working to build a space at the intersection of the two. The depth of teaching, length of service, and freedom of expression are all areas that we carefully consider to avoid being an insular community that does not grow.

If you do this right, then when a non-believer comes who is open, they may be touched by God and be saved. When a believer comes, they will be fed important truths from the Word of God and continual refreshment of the Spirit. Figuratively speaking, the Sunday service is the "living room" of the house – the place where you welcome people to your family.

But remember the Tabernacle. We need more than a Courtyard. We need also to build spaces that are more like the Tent of Meeting. Or think about it like a house. A house with only a living room would be very constricting to those who live there every day. Private spaces like bedrooms and offices are essential in order to dwell there. This is the second piece of the encounter system – creating spaces which are presumed to be inhabited exclusively by believers where we can go deeper with God.

Some of these spaces exist as part of the other systems of the church: Growth small groups, for example, create a pathway for people to journey with God and should become increasingly deep along the way. Likewise, Ministry small groups are places where people can get vulnerable about the challenges they are facing. Groups, however, are intentionally smaller and focused so a complete encounter system should include one or more corporate opportunities to go deeper.

## DEEPER ENCOUNTER SERVICE

One way to meet this need is to create a special service, one night a week, which is intentionally longer, deeper, and more ministry-oriented. Instead of half an hour of worship, you might have an hour. Or, instead of a short message, you may invite special speakers who can really explode a topic over an hour or more. Instead of a brief invitation for prayer at the end of service, you might have extended ministry time. You wouldn't do all these things together, but they all provide opportunities for the Holy Spirit to work more deeply than on the Sunday service schedule.

Other possibilities include inviting people to minister to one another or having a ministry team work the crowd proactively. You might open up more free expression in testimony or worship – although honoring God's presence always involves healthy boundaries as we discussed in Chapter 6. Perhaps you conduct a "Night of Worship," where there is no teaching but just extended times of worship, laced with prayer and ministry. Regardless of the exact format, these kinds of changes are intended to open things up and create an atmosphere where God can do more for the family.

To be clear, I'm not making a contrast here between a Sunday service where we try to limit God's presence and another night where we don't. In both cases we are talking about cultivating the atmosphere of His presence. But the depth of encounter makes it look a little different. To follow the analogy of a home, when we have guests over, we prepare the living room to make them feel welcomed and comfortable, but when they retire to the guest room, we have prepared it to be warm and personal.

## ENCOUNTER CONFERENCES

Conferences draw people together who are hungry for

more. If you invite people who are well known for supernatural ministry and their closeness to God, it creates an atmosphere of expectation where anything can happen. These are often the kinds of environments where dramatic life-changing miracles happen. If you want your church to really be an encounter-based church, you need to have them at least occasionally. Doing it well can take a lot of effort to put on, but it can also catapult your church forward in a way that almost nothing else can.

An ideal conference centers around several ministers known for their spirituality, and an anointed and well-known worship team. This will create draw as well as hunger. One common model for a conference is a Friday night session with two to four sessions on Saturday, as well as some "track" opportunities where people can grow in specific topics. A meal or two provides networking moments to grow relationships, and sometimes there is a follow-up session on Sunday morning if your keynote speaker is still in town. If your church hosts the conference, the core attendance would come from your church, but speakers will draw many others. Make sure to invite these guests to come back on Sunday. The growth of your church may be hiding there.

## PRAYER

Prayer is an essential part of the Encounter System, but also the Growth System. Put directly, without prayer your church will not grow. You are in a spiritual battle for people's souls. Prayer can often feel like labor, or can be boring for the uninitiated, but my life experience has shown me clearly how much a difference there is between when you pray and when you don't. The prayers you don't pray are the miracles that don't happen, the divine appointments you don't meet and the God-encounters you don't have.

*The prayers you don't pray are the miracles that don't happen.*

I first became convinced of this when

I read the classic book *Fresh Wind, Fresh Fire* by Jim Cymbala. In that book he talks about the powerful prayer meetings that launched the Brooklyn Tabernacle. Because of this book, when I really started chasing God, the weekly prayer meeting became a "do-not-miss" part of my week. It was around that time that I met a young lady who was an atheist. I began to reach out to her, and my prayer partner began to pray for her salvation. I was doing the right things in terms of witnessing to her but as my intercessor friend prayed consistently, we began to see inexplicable miracles that opened this lady's heart to Jesus and led to her dramatic salvation... and eventually to her becoming my wife! The prayers themselves were not dramatic but they were consistent, and they changed a life. That's the difference prayer makes.

## INTERCESSORY PRAYER

Intercessory prayer is the kind of prayer that most Spirit-filled believers are familiar with. These meetings can create a red-hot atmosphere which I believe makes them very powerful. It also tends to make them, by nature, a small group activity. For the most part, there simply isn't room for more than a few people to pray intensely together at once.

For this reason, I suggest that you appoint someone with a gift and passion for prayer, and whom you trust to lead an intercessory team. This can include backroom prayer before and during service, and also weekly prayer over key church needs. Because of the nature of this kind of prayer, some guidelines are important for those you recognize as intercessors in your church:

1. **Focus on Jesus**, not the enemy. Sometimes people will fixate on rebuking the devil. This gives him glory and can even empower him. Lift Jesus over everything and He will rebuke the devil.

2. **Pray in alignment with leadership**. We don't pray out our frustrations, i.e. "God, we ask you that our pastor would repent and rend his heart!" While you will likely see

areas where your church or leaders need to grow, a public setting is not an appropriate way to raise them. You can talk to leadership directly or pray for them privately. In public, though, intercessors are trusted to pray in accordance with the direction of leadership.

3. **Share the Floor**. Sometimes intercessory people can pray for a really extended period all at once, or too many times. This takes the energy away from others. It can even discourage the team from wanting to meet. It's important that we always demonstrate awareness of others. This is also why we keep the meeting small.

4. **Stay on Topic**. It's not constructive if the prayer time wanders into random needs or outlying/unknown requests. We want to keep each intercessory meeting focused on the items at hand. Of course there are those moments where the Spirit leads into a sudden topic or depth that we follow, but drawing the team into a potpourri of subjects which are unrelated or they are disconnected from can really break the Spirit's flow.

The key for great intercessory prayer meetings are that the meeting has a leader who keeps it focused on the needs of 1) the church body and 2) on Jesus. We don't generally rebuke the enemy, we adore the Lord. We pray into the positive, not the negative. We declare and contend for the promises of God as they apply to our community and context.

CORPORATE PRAYER SERVICE

A corporate prayer service is a way we can engage the entire body in prayer. It is intended to draw a much broader group of people than just those who are uniquely gifted and called to intercessory prayer.

This meeting could be done as a regular mid-week prayer and worship service. In our church's prayer meeting, we do a worship set of about half an hour, which transitions to guided prayer led by the pastor or other prayer leader for about the same length, with the team still playing in the background. The worship part of the meeting feeds your hungry people as well as attracts people who need a refresh that week. The prayer component gives you a place to pray corporately over the needs of your church and community. It also allows people to exercise their gifts in a safe environment, for example praying in tongues or praying over one another more freely. Our church has done this with great effect, often having as much as 20% of our Sunday attendance at the meeting.

The guidelines for a prayer meeting are similar to the Sunday service, but with more interactivity. The meeting is led by the pastor or other senior leader. If you're the pastor, I recommend giving each of your key leaders a chance to lead a prayer meeting, but it is important that you personally be invested in prayer if you want your church to grow.

After the encounter-oriented worship set, the leader leads several different styles of prayer as he or she feels led. The goal is to activate and engage the body in prayer without letting someone pull the focus away for their pet concerns or personal message. These styles include:

**Adoration Prayer:** Many people have not been exposed to adoration prayer, but it is the most common form of prayer the Psalms and a very powerful way to set the atmosphere in the room. This is when you tell the Lord how wonderful He is. You can pick a theme and expound upon it just like you would if you were encouraging another person. It can include giving thanks but is primarily focused on exalting God. Naturally we tend to focus on the concerns of the day and look down, but when we look up at who God is, these things get put in their proper perspective and our faith rises. Several minutes of heartfelt adoration by the leader can be incredibly powerful to open a prayer meeting.

**Topical Prayer.** This is when you or someone you designate leads prayer for a specific topic, i.e faith, the lost, provision. I recommend that you have anyone who leads an important function in your church pray over their function, and also receive prayer from others during this time. The main thing is that topical prayers should be corporate in nature, pertaining to the whole church body, not specific individuals or things beyond your reach.

**Prayer Queue.** One way to engage everyone in prayer is to invite them to give 30-60 second prayers on the mic. People line up or take turns. You can either set a topic related to the church, or you can open it up by inviting people to read and pray a Scripture. Cue a couple of your leaders to go first to set the tone.

**Prayer for Each Other.** Ask everyone to get into groups of three or four, and share their concerns with one another for prayer. These are some of the most enjoyable times in prayer, as people get to unload their burdens and also have the joy of encouraging others. Alternatively you can have your prayer ministry team come up front and invite people to come forward for prayer. Each has its own advantages.

**Prophetic Prayer.** I am a strong believer in both God's power to heal as well as prophetic ministry. If you have seasoned and trusted prophetic people in your Body, then the prayer meeting is a great opportunity to allow them to pray and minister at large. Someone receiving a well-tuned and targeted word can be incredibly impactful for everyone. It's also a great time to invite prayer for healing for specific illnesses as led by the Spirit. Prophetic healing is when you focus on a specific issue identified by the Spirit to pray for on that night.

**Prayer Cards.** At least once a month we bring our church prayer requests to the prayer meeting (on cards), spread them on a table, and have everyone come and take one or more to pray over them. This allows us to pray over many requests quickly and engages the Body in a healthy way in the needs of our community.

There are many ways you can mix, match, and tailor these basic themes to keep your prayer meeting interesting as well as follow the leading of the Spirit. The main thing is that it is a time for us to pray as a family, for the family. During our entire meeting, we keep the music going in the background, and often finish with a chorus together. We also start on time and finish on time, every time—exactly one hour. This keeps people energized in the meeting and motivated to come again.

## WAITING ON THE LORD

My good friend Dan Bohi has a ministry which has profoundly affected the entire Nazarene church through powerful healing and revival teaching. He asked the Lord last year why he had not yet seen Him move in greater measure and the Lord told him, "You've done everything but wait on me." The Bible does indicate this:

> But they that **wait upon the Lord** shall renew their strength; they shall mount up with wings as eagles; they shall run, and not be weary; and they shall walk, and not faint. (Isa 40:31)
> I **waited** patiently for the Lord; he turned to me and heard my cry. (Psa 40:1)

With this in mind, Dan and his team held a week-long series of meetings he called "the waiting." During this time, they primarily sat in the presence of the Lord together. They began each meeting with an anointed worship leader who knew how to respond to the Spirit and lead prophetically. As the time extended, they would move into a time of waiting, sometimes with music, sometimes without, allowing Him space to come.

Over the course of hours, as they honored His presence, it got stronger and stronger, building up to a profound encounter. Just like a quiet time before the Lord opens us up to a personal encounter, a corporate time of quiet and waiting can create the atmosphere of corporate encounter. Think of how difficult it is to have a conversation when someone else is always talking. I think that sometimes when we hold corporate prayer we forget to listen. Holding a waiting meeting reverses the direction and makes room for Him to speak.

I once experienced a moment of what I can only call Holy

Silence in a meeting. In this moment an awesome sense of reverence came into the room and as people honored it, it became deeper and more profound, and finally it concluded with a powerful prophetic word for the body. These are the kinds of things that can happen when we learn how to wait on the Lord.

## WHAT ABOUT PROPHETIC MINISTRY?

As a prophetic person who has ministered in a variety of settings, I have strong feelings about the importance of the prophetic for cultivating encounter with God. In fact, Paul specifically highlights personal prophetic ministry as a critical component of bringing people into the Kingdom of God (1 Corinthians 14:25). High level prophetic ministry by mature leaders is absolutely life changing and, according to the Bible, not just something for the back office.

Specifically, a word of knowledge given to an individual in a public setting in an appropriate way can not only change that person's life but can change the lives of many people who are in the room – that's what happened to me. My passion for God was ignited when I saw high level prophetic ministry in action on someone else. I realized that God really did know the number of hairs on my head and loved me in a personal way beyond my understanding. I was hooked. I believe this is exactly the kind of thing Paul had in mind.

On the other hand, a lot of things can go wrong when we open the door to the prophetic, especially in a corporate meeting. This understandably causes many pastors to shy away from it. But the real question is: do you want to have a swimming pool that only has a shallow end? Only children enjoy swimming in a pool with no deep end. On the other hand, when you have a deep end, people will drown if you don't take proper safety precautions. Prophetic ministry is like this.

To fully answer how we can conduct healthy prophetic ministry in the church would require a book of its own. I wrote the *School of the Spirit* partly as a way of addressing that question, and I encourage you to check it out, but I want to offer a few framing thoughts here.

First, I want to distinguish between personal prophetic ministry, and all of the revelatory-related activities that are sometimes filed under "the prophetic." Welcoming "the prophetic" is not synonymous with allowing unbalanced people to roam around your congregation telling people what they heard from God. Or allowing people to grandstand about personal dreams or revelations. It's about inviting trusted leaders to hear from God and minister to others in that context.

Additionally, any revelation or prophecy intended for the whole body should be carefully prayed over by the leadership team before any larger audience hears it. While this is simply common sense for anyone who has ever run an organization, most of the time a church either allows an "open mic" kind of atmosphere or they shut down corporate prophecy altogether. The open mic often becomes a venue for someone who is not otherwise a leader to get time on the mic either to gain attention or vent an issue. Even when a word is accurate, without proper handling, it may not be easily applicable.

*Revelation is given by God to help us steer the ship, grow the church, and invite Jesus more.*

As a prophetic voice in my community, when I have a dream or word pertaining to the direction of my church, I submit it to the pastor. He is the leader of the place my family and I are honored to be part of. I do so in such a way that does not make him feel like he is being held at gunpoint. Revelation is given by God to help us steer the ship, grow the church, and invite Jesus more. There are times when a word may be encouraging to the whole body, but it is his choice on whether he wants to share it or not, how, and at what time. I know the boundaries of his vision and what he is comfortable with. The entire endeavor is based on trust.

These are self-evident parameters of what it means to minister "decently and *in order*" (1 Cor. 14:40), not just in the prophetic, but in any context. In that sense stewarding the prophetic is not any different from stewarding your own gifts of worship, teaching, or any other talent in the Body. I think we confuse ourselves because prophetic revelation is directly from God—but then leadership is also ordained by God, which is the counterbalance. It is destructive to use a word directly from God to undermine the leadership He has put in place. Remember, "the one who prophesies speaks to people for their strengthening, encouraging and comfort." (1 Cor 14:3) We build up, we don't tear down. And as it regards the church, prayer is the most important part of the prophetic. I have to do more than give words, I steward them by praying into them.

At the same time, I believe that the prophetic is not just for the platform. It is for every believer. However, just like giving your child a power tool, you don't simply turn it loose with no instructions or purpose. Again, we need to move past the hard dichotomy we've been in of all-or-nothing. We also need to put shaping and practice into honing the prophetic. Those interested in ministry should be led by seasoned leaders to practice their gifts in a safe environment and be vetted before being released to minister prophetically in the Body. The answer to misuse is not disuse, but training for proper use.

*Only the one who is faithful with little should be given more.*

In general, we should treat prophetic ministry the same way we treat other kinds of ministry – only the one who is faithful with little should be given more. It can be all too easy to allow someone with gifting to skip steps to ministry, but history and experience shows that will lead to people getting hurt. If someone won't serve, take direction, or go through the same steps of training as everyone else has to, they are not safe for ministry in your congregation. The gift may be real, but teachability is the license.

With that said, I believe Paul's guidance in 1 Corinthians 14 makes it clear that we should welcome the mature prophetic with the right boundaries in our services, even and especially the ones where we expect unbelievers to be present. If we are handling revelation well, it should open the door to dramatic encounter which can change lives and propel people towards Jesus in a radical way.

# The Growth System

The Growth System consists of two primary avenues where we expect personal growth to occur: service and education. Service is where we grow through doing, and education is where we grow through learning. You need tactics that will encourage people down both of these paths.

A traditional church has components that are intended for growth, such as Sunday school, Bible studies, and women's or men's events. The problem is that these do not create a logical pathway of growth. A potpourri of non-directed activities does not grow your church personally or numerically. They mostly maintain community over a common connection point, which actually has a tendency to create stasis. We must always be reaching new people or we stagnate and die. Remember, it's human nature to want to see the same people we are comfortable with all of the time rather than expanding our circle of influence. This is why most studies or activities are really about attendance more than objectives.

Practically speaking, this means that you need to look at every activity your church has to evaluate whether or not it is a tool of growth or a tool of stagnation. Consider every activity that you do or are considering doing from the perspective of inputs and outputs. The input is the type of person you are looking for and the output is the step of growth you are hoping they will gain from it. Too frequently church programs have neither of these: We invite people to do something like a Bible study, but there is no particular target audience and no particular desired result. As leaders we need to put our energy toward creating and promoting activities that are invitational, inclusive and have a destination in mind.

## SERVICE

One natural tendency as church leaders is to focus on education as the primary pathway of personal growth, but Jesus had a different method: He invited the disciples to follow Him, taught them in parallel, and then gave them opportunities to put their training into practice. To build a healthy and engaged body, you have to provide opportunities and pathways for service and engagement, not just pathways for education.

I've gone on this journey myself. When I was accepted into a Ph.D program in ministry, I was very excited about the possibilities. But as I prayed into it, I felt that God was showing me that if I wanted to have a real impact with my life, I would have to focus on making my knowledge useful and practical to others, rather than on gaining more.

Service is important because building up your knowledge can create an illusion of significance. If we don't learn through taking action, **we are actually learning not to take action**! Knowledge actually becomes a substitute for action. We start to think that doctrine, answers, or "knowing truth" is the end of Christianity. But as James says, "faith without *works* is dead" (James 1:17). Living deeds are supposed to follow our living faith.

Furthermore, without service our ideas never get tested. I remember having very clear ideas about how people change until I worked with men on the streets and got to observe how it really worked. Once I put my hand to the plow, I had to make significant adjustments in my theology. It's the testing our of our ideas that allows us to refine them.

Service moves our focus outside ourselves to others. Not everyone is ready to lead others, but everyone can serve others including the leadership! Along with that, service creates a sense of shared ownership. When you are responsible for something, it takes you from spectator to participant. This is so important for a church. The more co-owners and co-laborers you have, the more momentum you will have as an organization. A church can't run on the pastor alone, or even on the leadership team. It has to be carried by the Body.

Lastly, a culture of service takes the focus off doctrine, which tends to only interest the committed few and can be divisive. Instead, service puts the cultural focus on **shared goals**. The more you serve and push for shared goals, the less important the peripheral areas become. Everyone can help set the church up, regardless of their view on the End Times. And when setup is over, we all feel united.

## CREATING OWNERS

In a traditional church model, it's common for people to focus on pet projects while delegating everything else to the pastor and paid staff. This can make a pastor very tired, very quickly. To be successful, you want to build a pipeline of co-owners.

*Every job you delegate well is a partner you create.*

This means giving people a stake in the success of the church. Not everyone wants the same size stake, and not everyone is qualified for the size stake they want, but the goal should always be to create a team of co-laborers around you. Every job you delegate well is a partner you create. Additionally, service roles give people a sense of personal ownership, even agreement. They create a culture of work and unity, rather than the critical armchair-quarterback culture that pervades many churches.

At the same time, there is a limit to this concept. Once you discover the buy-in that serving can create, it's tempting to create more and more work to provide more and more jobs! This will appear to succeed for a while, and then people will burn themselves out and disappear. Volunteers love to do jobs that have to be done, but they resent doing jobs that don't need to be done. Therefore, make sure to apply Occam's Razor to everything you ask people to do: if something is not necessary, do not do it. Also consider the Golden Rule of Leadership: If you would not to do the task, do not ask others to do it. This will keep your culture of service from burning people out.

Remember church is about people. When you put too much energy into what needs to be done, you start to be drawn away from the purpose of why you are doing them – which is to welcome people and host the presence of God. The 80/20 rule should apply here as well: 80 percent of your focus and energy should be toward people and ministry, while 20 percent of your energy should be going toward the things that need to be done in order for that ministry to happen. When that gets reversed, people's lives will start to fall through the cracks, and the stories that come back to you will be hard to hear

Of course, people who have a calling and a passion for a certain task can find joy in doing things that others don't—because it is an expression of an important part of who they are. At the same time, not everyone is going to have a passion to do all the basic tasks it takes to run the Sunday service. This can lead to an imbalance where the one lady who has a passion for kids ministry is staffing it every single weekend until she burns herself out. To avoid this, we create a positive culture of service where we engage people who may not have a life passion in a specific area but love to contribute.

*When you celebrate those who serve, it creates a positive culture.*

The first part of this positive culture is role modeling. You and your leaders should have service roles to show that it's something enjoyable, not something that should be avoided. Secondly, it's important to have **celebration**. When you celebrate those who serve, it creates a positive culture. Look for opportunities to celebrate those who serve. An occasional event or meal just for them reminds them that they are part of something bigger, and appreciated.

The goal is to create the feeling that serving is a fun and normal part of church life. My kids all have roles in the church, and I can say for a fact that their roles have made them co-owners in a way that I don't see in other youth. A positive culture of service can be really life changing for people.

It's also a good screen for people. If someone is not willing to serve, then they are not good material for higher levels of leadership. Jesus says, "Whoever wants to become great among you must be your servant" (Matthew 20:26). Follow that rule and it will spare you the pain of people who want important positions for the wrong reasons.

At the same time, many potential leaders will choose to serve specifically because they are hoping for future ministry leadership roles. They may not feel called to the parking team, but they see the need and do the role because they support you, and are hoping for future opportunities. It's important to reward these people for doing the right thing by looking for other doors where they get to express more of their ministry identity. When future leaders learn that parking team is the doorway to advancement, you'll never have an understaffed parking team.

## YOUR EVENT STAFF

Every Sunday, your church is running a pretty large event. In order for it to be excellent, you need all of the same kinds of elements in place that would be present for any other large scale event, such as a convention or concert. Every role on your Service team is essential to attracting and retaining people. To get this going, you need roles to deploy people into and a pipeline to continually staff those roles. Here are some of the areas of service to look at:

- **Worship.** The worship team is the heart of the church. You need a leader that is anointed and has leadership qualities. Don't settle until you have the right person. People with musical talent and a passion for God in worship can serve here.

- **Children.** The biggest service need in a growing and

excellent church is in children's church. Parents look much more closely at their children's experience than they do their own. You need separate classes by age and lots of volunteers. Putting the moms back there all the time is a loss for everyone. Try to avoid it by adding younger or older people there to serve and creating a rotation system.

- **Security.** A security team is essential in the 21$^{st}$ century. There are trained individuals in almost every church who would love to have this responsibility. Get them trained so they can be excellent. A medical person may also be a good add-in here for emergencies.

- **Greeting/Ushers.** Greeters are the warm personalities that are the first point of contact in your church. Ushers are responsible for ensuring that people have a pleasant experience including seating, offering, and communion. They should look nice and represent you well, and should also be coordinated with security.

- **Production.** In the old days, there was just one guy in the sound booth. Today, you need to think bigger. You need to think about sound, lighting, and any projected presentation in support of the speaker, at minimum. Many churches video record for online outlets. Production provides some of the most essential roles in the church today.

- **Creative & Marketing.** There need to be people dedicated to your church's presentation and marketing, whatever the level you have margin for. This includes your website, Instagram feed, email communications, and the photo and video to support them. It may also include things like merchandise, logo design, style, other aspects of branding that would appear on stationery, gifts, connection cards, prayer cards, invitations, presentations, etc.

- **Hospitality.** Your guests should be welcomed with a great experience, which today often includes coffee. You may also have other hospitality needs such as food for those serving, an info booth, helpers at the door or parking lot, seasonal decorations, etc.

- **Facility Readiness.** Every church needs people whose job it is to make the facility ready before use. This can be as simple as coming in before service and checking bathrooms, carpet, etc. Or, if you are in a portable church situation, this could be a major service component.

These are the kinds of roles that make the Sunday service work. You don't have to have this exact set of teams. You might find that based on your needs, you can combine some functions, or you may need more. Look at every function of the church, including the ones you are doing, and ask yourself "Is there someone I could delegate this to?"

Of course, some functions are much more important than others. Some areas may require simply people who are willing while others might require you to raise up someone deeply trusted or capable. Giving out both kinds of jobs gives people the opportunity to become more invested, and it also sets the culture of service in the church.

### AVOIDING BURNOUT AND BURNDOWN

The beauty of these serving opportunities is that, if you don't know them already, there are usually people in your congregation who are gifted in these areas. If you give them vision and good leadership, they would most likely love to serve at church in these ways as long as they are valued and managed well. The caveat is that while responsibilities that are managed well create ownership and buy-in, responsibilities that are managed poorly create disaffected people.

Some church growth resources make what I believe is a mistake in pushing the idea of service so far that it supplants the personal aspects of ministry. If almost all of the roles in the church are directly connected to the work it takes to run its own activities, then few of them lead people down the path to helping others grow personally. A healthy church celebrates those who serve while keeping the focus on life change in the people who we are doing all of the service for.

Anytime we have service roles, an important part of our stewardship is making sure that we're not working someone into the ground unintentionally. I had a close friend who once who worked 10-hour days in the sound booth as a service to his church. There were only a small number of men willing to work like this on their day off, and so it was very hard for my friend to quit with a clean conscience. By the time he did, he felt mistreated and unappreciated by the church. His responsibility needed to be redesigned by a manager so that it could be done joyfully over the long haul, not put on a burnout schedule. Kids church and worship are other areas where this is common.

Christians are unique because the Spirit inside of us gives us a love for service, but that same love can often cause us to work beyond what is sustainable without telling anyone. Because of this, sometimes the first time leaders will notice someone's burnout is not until they leave your church. They probably complained to close friends first, and maybe told you a nice story when they left, but if they were working themselves to death, you can be assured that's the underlying cause. I will never forget the young girl who we later found out was crying herself to sleep for months because of how hard she was working, and no-one knew. For many of us on the leadership team, the first sign we had was when she not only left the church, but the faith. Completely heartbreaking.

Apparently, the people serving under King Solomon had a similar kind of issue because the first time we hear about their discontent is after he is dead. Then when their complaint was not addressed, they were so upset they left the country! (1 Kings 12) To avoid this, you should ruthlessly apply the golden rule to your service roles: How would this service responsibility make me feel if I were in a similar life position as those serving in it?

Unfortunately, I could go on with story after story of people who have gotten burned out serving in church, but which I believe were avoidable. There are signs and symptoms common across churches. When a talented leader steps back to pursue other things, there is a high chance that they have either burned themselves out or that their contribution and gift has not been properly honored. The *culture of honor* is what I believe is the antidote to these scenarios. It's been said that people want to be *seen, celebrated,* and *soothed.* When people are seen for the fullness of who they are, celebrated for what they contribute, and soothed from the challenges they experience, they will stay.

Part of passing this test is not creating unnecessary work. Remember the 80/20 rule. You need to assess honestly when "good enough" is "good enough." You are dealing with volunteers, so think and plan with optimization in mind. When you ask people to do things which they believe are unnecessary, it creates dissatisfaction and undermines your culture of service. On the other hand, when you give essential responsibilities to people, it makes them feel important.

Scheduling is an important consideration as well. Scheduling on a rotation solves an important problem to help prevent burnout, but it also creates a lot of overhead for your leaders to build and maintain the schedule. Even with tools designed for this purpose, it can easily become a major task to create schedules and follow up with people to ensure they are responding and are present. For this reason, I think it's important to strike a balance between faithful people who want to serve regularly, and scheduling to ensure the regulars are not overloaded.

As needs for scheduling grows, I recommend centralizing this task to a paid admin person so that your team leaders can focus on their actual job more than the scheduling. This is a low-cost hire that can be part time. You can also have simple rotations or build redundancy so that there are other people who can handle things in case of an absence to reduce the need for schedules. Creating a list of on-call substitutes for prayer team, greeters, kids church, and hospitality (who do not serve regularly but only as substitutes) can solve a lot of problems. I recommend updating this seasonally.

## GROWTH TRACK

If the first part of personal growth is serving, the second part is education and training. Once someone has had a transformative encounter with the Lord, it is important to create pathways of growth for them so they do not stagnate or slide back. Especially if a person has just made a decision for Christ, you want to be able to jump on that immediately and give them their next growth step.

I suggest creating an interlocking series of classes or groups designed to establish foundations, and then other classes or groups which train and empower people for Spirit-filled ministry and life. I recommend that you deploy them on a semester calendar either in a small group or classroom format, depending on your context. They should be as interactive and practical as possible. More on the details of how small groups can work for you in the chapter on the Ministry system.

**Foundations**. The first piece needed is a Christian Foundations course. It should cover the elementary teachings of the faith such as salvation, baptism, the authority of Scripture, and the Holy Spirit. (Heb 6:1). A Foundations course serves multiple purposes. For brand new believers, the first few months after someone commits to the Lord are a crucial time where they are incredibly open to direction. God can do a great deal in these moments. It's also a time when a new believer's ties to the world need to be severed, and their understanding of self and life direction need to be reshaped. I have developed a Bible study, *Come Follow Me,* which can be used either in a foundations class or as a one-on-one tool.

New believers are like new pottery: the closer to the decision moment you can reach them, the wetter the clay. It's crucial that people receive a fresh foundation as close to the moment of salvation as possible so you don't lose them. In fact, in the case of a truly radical conversion, a Foundations course alone is probably not enough. We want to see that person baptized quickly, filled with the Holy Spirit quickly, and sharing their testimony with friends quickly. These activities establish the foundation for their new life before the concrete sets.

They may also need discipleship if they are going back to a challenging life situation which could flood out their new faith. A great leader told me once that "The way you start is the way you finish." Look for the opportunity to connect them to a mature believer who can dedicate time to them right away help them get launched in the right direction. Have one of your key leaders dedicated to administrating the touchback components for new believers since it is such a precious job before the Lord.

Foundations is not just for new believers, though. For rededicating believers or those with some Christian background, Foundations can ensure that they do not have any holes in their basic beliefs that need to be addressed. Foundations can also help new members get on board with the way your church sees and emphasizes things, even if they're already committed Christians. When a mature leader from another background goes through your Foundations and aligns with them, you have a great opportunity for long-term relationship.

Additionally, if seasoned believers do not go through or do not align, it helps them self-select out. Self-selection is always the ideal way to manage people's expectations. If someone wants a greater role but they are not ready, give them a step that will help make them ready. If they don't take the step, they are self-selecting out of the pipeline, which helps both of you in a painless way.

**Freedom.** Foundations class is a basis for right thinking and living, but often times believers are carrying a lot of baggage even if they do not know it. You should have a course, group, or seminar weekend in place specifically to help with this. The classic tool for this purpose is Cleansing Streams, first popularized through Jack Hayford's ministry, but there are many others with their own flavor. Gateway Church, the Vineyard, and Church of the Highlands also have well designed tracks with this in mind that you can adapt. The key is that somehow you create a safe environment for believers to look at deep personal and past issues, and invite the Holy Spirit to minister to them.

There is no doubt that this kind of ministry can become a little messy – you may find yourself dealing with and removing demonic strongholds. Yet Cleansing Streams and others have demonstrated that this kind of ministry can be done in a structured, user-friendly way, and can lead to massive acceleration in a person's life. This is also a logical time to invite people to become filled with the Holy Spirit if they have not done so before, and get them educated on how the Holy Spirit empowers them to live victoriously.

**Outreach and Mission.** Perhaps the most important thing that every church member needs to do is understand how to (and how not to) share their faith. This is especially true if they have received training before from the aggressive kind of outreach style we mentioned in Chapter 4 that has dominated American evangelism. We need to learn how to share Jesus in ways that are *naturally supernatural*, how to recognize when He is working, and how to bring Him into the normal everyday situations of our lives, both with people we are close to and people we will only cross paths with one time. John Wimber's classic *Power Evangelism* remains relevant today to help build this culture. If your church is just starting to think outwardly, *The Difference Maker* by Nelson Searcy is an outstanding resource designed specifically to help make outreach normal.

**Spirit-Filled Ministry Training.** John Wimber famously asked one of his first pastors, "When do we get to do the stuff?" By this he meant walk in the miraculous gifts of the Holy Spirit like the apostles did in Acts. The pastor's lack of an answer led Wimber on a quest which eventually led to starting the Vineyard denomination, with the emphasis that all can minister the gifts of the Holy Spirit.

Sadly, still today, most pastors would not be able to give a good answer for John Wimber's question. For some, this is because they simply do not have any experience or background themselves. Others feel constrained by the church body or denomination they are a part of. Some have experience with the supernatural but have decided that the risks associated outweigh the benefits. They are concerned about how this kind of ministry can be abused, especially as it relates to people who are just discovering the Lord. I think that in the minds of many, Spirit-filled expression simply becomes a distraction that costs more than it is worth – something that people love, but which doesn't really help build the church.

I am glad to say that you can empower people in Spirit-filled ministry without opening the door to chaos – at least not more chaos than you face pastoring any other area of your church! I once had the opportunity to spend time with a famous leader who had started multiple movements which handled the Spirit especially well. I asked him how they were able to do it so successfully, and he simply said "discipleship."

Proper training and discipleship is the key to healthy Spirit-filled ministry. Imagine the results if we just let some random guy jump on the soundboard. It would be a disaster. Yet in some Spirit-filled environments, they do the equivalent with the Holy Spirit. As a senior leader it can be easy to see functioning in spiritual gifts as merely something that "the people want," but it's better to recognize that the gifts are power tools which allow God to touch His people much more deeply and powerfully.

When we train our people to use them well, they are not sources of chaos but tools for explosive growth. I think about two young ladies who were healed of auto-immune diseases through ministry at our church. Their lives are so much better, they are fully connected to the church, and they have much more energy to contribute. With training, modeling, and discipleship, you can have an environment in your church that is supernatural but not ungoverned or weird.

This is why I wrote a manual, the *School of the Spirit,* which we used to train our prayer team and has been adopted by other churches facing similar challenges. It is designed to be run in a small group format, with one hour of teaching and one hour of interactive prayer ministry. This became a great community builder for us because it combines teaching with interaction about how to minister the Holy Spirit in a way that edifies your church.

**Leadership.** Since your goal is to produce leaders, giving people a vehicle where they can receive explicit training will accelerate your church. The worldview of leadership is not natural for most people. They will catch it as you live it out in your church, but you also need to give them language and paradigms. Oswald Sanders' classic *Spiritual Leadership* can be a great tool for this purpose, as can a number of popular podcasts led by famous Christian leaders.

Use a Leadership class as a vehicle to communicate and train people on the things that will make them successful at your church as well as in the rest of life. For the younger crowd, you might try something like *Adulting 101.* Many in the younger generation were simply deprived of the basic tools and perspectives they need to be successful. Giving them these basic tools can be life changing.

**Cultural Engagement.** If our ultimate goal is to change the world for Jesus, people need training that will help them down that path. The natural orientation as a pastor is for growth to only address explicitly spiritual activities of life rather than to include all of life. But you can change your community if you build and activate leaders who know how to live and act outside of the four walls. The end result of personal growth should be leaders with the capacity to build the Kingdom of God. That's why we need to teach cultural engagement components as well.

As our society separates more and more from its Biblical foundations, people are in increasing need of structured teaching on how to think about contemporary life issues. They also need help on how to apply truth to their lives. This has led to the advent of "Biblical Worldview" as a topic for study, which helps Christians to think about societal topics in a Christian way.

As we help people think about societal issues from a Biblical angle, it's important to hold discussions about how to apply them more directly. Pastors often avoid these touchy kinds of topics because of the potential for controversy, but when you do it as part of a track with those who are already committed, and you do it without being too pushy, it can actually build greater unity in your church body. To have the biggest impact, it's important when you touch these topics to keep the discussion rooted in the Bible, and to avoid directly addressing politics of the moment. *Counter Culture* by David Platt covers controversial topics in a contemporary way and is designed for small groups. *The Truth Project* by *Focus on the Family* is also a good resource. There are other good resources, but many are geared toward a highly educated crowd, rather than the social media generation.

Biblical Worldview is a great starting point, but we want to make sure that we move from just right thinking to right action. Ultimately, we want to build up and send out people who are *doing* Christianity in a transformational way. *Made to Flourish* is a ministry which produces a lot of practical resources which are designed to help activate people into Kingdom Callings.

They work closely with *Acton Institute* which resources Christian leaders to think Biblically about the world, and holds great conferences each year for this purpose. They have produced *For the Life of the World* and *Rethink Missions.*

I have gone over several core areas that make up a well-developed Growth Track, but they are certainly not exclusive. Depending on your unique focus as a church, and the availability of qualified leaders, there are many other topics that could be considered in this track, including things like Missions, Old and New Testament, or Pastoral Care. Creating a well-run growth track fills many needs in your congregation. It helps fill a need that many people feel for generalized Bible study, replacing it with focused Biblical education on a topic. It gives people who want to go deeper, a direction and way to do that. Also, leaders in your church who have a gift and desire to teach, once they are trusted members of your team, can have a great outlet for their passion.

## NEXT STEPS

In order to create an effective connection from the Sunday service to the growth track, you need great on-ramps and messaging at your Sunday service to encourage people toward those on-ramps. Instead of the traditional membership class, many churches today employ a repeating series of welcome sessions that introduce people to the church, refresh them on the basics of the faith, and direct them into service roles. The one our church uses lasts 3 weeks on a repeating basis, and is held in an adjoining room after the Sunday service so that people who are ready to get more involved with our church have a direct opportunity to do so.

This series of courses forms a bridge from the Sunday service to the rest of the church life, so it is a very critical piece. Many churches give this the very descriptive name "Next Steps," so I'm going to use that term throughout the book. But regardless of what you call your course, the basic orientation should include:

- **Background** about your church and leadership team. This helps people feel comfortable and get to know you better.

- **Christian Foundations.** The gospel can be shared a bit more directly and with more detail than you might have in the Sunday service. Along with this, you should review the most essential Christian beliefs, including the opportunity to be baptized if they never have been before.

- **Service Opportunities.** One of your main goals is to give people a next step in their growth and how to get involved. Identify for them any specific service opportunities open in the church, and groups or opportunities ideal for ministry or connection for newcomers.

- **Growth Groups.** Encourage people to jump into your sequence of growth classes or small groups as soon as the next session starts. This will help them go deeper in their personal discipleship and understanding, as well meet likeminded friends.

**Outreach Groups and Teams.** No one is better at outreach than people who have recently been reached. If you can help people get added to existing groups or be part of starting them, you will greatly energize your outreach.

Remember, the goal of this bridge component is to help people who are ready to connect more deeply to the body. They need to walk away with a clear pathway. It's even better if you facilitate their on-ramps by connecting them with specific leaders of teams, or groups, or adding them to a service opportunities email.

Be Spirit-led in discerning and recommending steps based on the kinds of talents and interests people put forward. Some people only want to belong while others want to contribute. Some are eager to lead while others need lots of time. Some would love to be part of your core ministry team if you showed them a pathway. Just don't rush anyone into ministry as that can cause conflict later, even disaster. Instead give them a series of opportunities to demonstrate if they are willing to follow you and attune to the values and style of your church. They need that experience as much as you do.

# The Ministry System

## OVERVIEW OF MINISTRY

It's easy to understand how church growth principles can end up sidelining what has traditionally been the *most* important part of a church: caring for each other and the world around you. In fact, many churches have gotten so good at attracting people that casualties from the lack of care go unseen. People coming in the front door distract us from those exiting from the back due to unmet needs.

This is where the Ministry System comes in. The Ministry System not only helps you close the backdoor, but it widens the front door. Many pastors burn themselves out from doing ministry, but when it's done right it's a huge blessing to your congregation.

The Growth system and the Ministry system are closely related, but exist for different reasons: the Growth System focuses on encouraging your church body to move forward in deeper levels of discipleship. Your Ministry System focuses on addressing the felt needs of the body. Another way to put it is, people come to church for Ministry, and then they must be led into Growth. While I have described them here in sequence, they really exist in parallel. People can and will have ministry needs before, during, and after their engagement in Growth activities. To prevent burnout and activate the gifts in your church body, it's important to have systems in place to meet them.

The Scriptural reality behind the Ministry System is that if we are faithful with little, we will be given much (Luke 16:10). Conversely, if we want to be given much, we must be faithful with little. That "little" is the people God sends to us. I remember when we launched our second church plant, I received prophetic ministry and the minister said, "You are wondering where the people are..." (which I was) and then they said, "…They are coming in February." When February came, two people discovered our church. I was underwhelmed at first. But then, as we got a good relationship going with them, it turned out they were very well connected and opened the doors for many others to find us. We had to be faithful with the two before we were given more.

Conversely, I remember one pastor who told us all that, "We're not a hospital church." We were dumbstruck. If we're not a hospital church, then what kind of church are we? There are so many Scriptures correcting this mentality, it's hardly necessary to present them, but suffice it to say that Jesus specifically says, "It is not the healthy who need a doctor, but the sick. I have not come to call the righteous, but sinners." (Mark 2:17). Better invite Dr. Jesus to practice in your church!

This pastor had gotten so far down the path of growth and success that he had forgotten the true essence of the Christian faith. Our love for the least is the proof-positive of our ability to care for the greatest. It is also a commandment (2 John 1:5), the way we know the love of God abides in us (1 John 3:14, 4:20), and the way the world sees Him through us "… if you love one another." (John 13:35).

At the same time, now that I've done a lot more ministry in my life, I do understand why a pastor would say that. Being entirely focused on meeting needs can literally collapse your life and stunt your church. Needy people can siphon the attention and resources away from leaders and those who are high capacity and ready to grow. This is an easy and quick trap that ministry-minded people fall into.

This is where systems helps us. They allow us to meet more needs without becoming swamped. A Ministry System facilitates the entire church body being engaged in meeting each other's needs (Eph 4:16) in ways that don't sink you or your ministry team. I'm glad to say that when done right, ministry and church growth are not opposites, but actually work together. When you help someone solve their challenging life issues, it creates a domino effect. The Bible describes this in many places. When the woman at the well was touched by Jesus, she went and told her whole town: "Come and see the man who told me everything I ever did" (John 4:29).

And she was not the only such story. The original disciples found Jesus this way. They got excited and told all of their friends. Great ministry is therefore the gateway for incredible growth because it leads to referrals. It is *meaningful* so news spreads. There is no more powerful witness for Jesus or for your church than a life that has truly been changed. Like-minded friends will beat the doors down to come in.

In secular marketing this is measured by something called the Net Promoter Score (NPS). The NPS is calculated by asking all of your clients the question, "How likely are you to refer our service to someone else?" People must reply with a number between 0 and 10. Those who reply with a number from 0-6 are classified as Detractors because they are likely to keep people from coming to your church. Those who reply with a 7 or 8 would be classified as Passives, because they are not likely to refer one way or the other. Those who respond with a 9 or a 10 are the golden ones and are classified as Promoters. These are the people you need to grow your church.

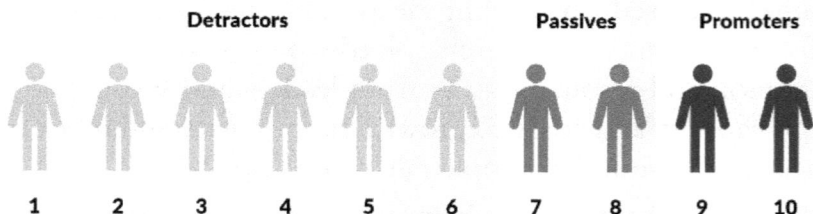

| Detractors | | | | | | Passives | | Promoters | |
|---|---|---|---|---|---|---|---|---|---|
| 1 | 2 | 3 | 4 | 5 | 6 | 7 | 8 | 9 | 10 |

The way you calculate the score is to subtract the percentage of Detractors from the percentage of Promoters, thus the name, Net Promoter Score.

One thing you'll notice right away is that the range of positive opinion that counts is much narrower than the range of negative opinion! This is because of human psychology. Our negative opinions and emotions are much more forceful than our positive ones. And even if something is mostly good, you end up talking more about those few things which kept it from being great. This means that cultivating a culture where people are so excited about your church that they are likely to refer it to their friends is hard, but important. In the beginning you can market your church and encourage people to refer it, and that will give some margin for a little while, but the primary way you generate referrals is by changing lives.

In the marketplace, when someone encounters a life-changing product, it's hard to get them to stop talking about it. As a personal example, after having four children, my wife's body was not able to regulate her temperature as well at night. She was waking up extremely overheated, so I searched hard for a solution. Finally I discovered the ChiliPad bed cooling system. We put it on the bed, and she started sleeping like a dream. Now I literally will refer it to anyone and everyone with sleeping problems to help them too! This is the kind of referral power you want working for you. Except that Jesus can change a life much more deeply than any product ever could.

Of course, the caveat is that you have to feel very confident referring the product or service to another person. Some life changing products are so fringe that even if they do change your life, you are unlikely to tell others because you are pretty sure they won't be able to relate or will think you are weird. This is why it is important that your service be mainstream enough to relate to those friends you want creating referrals. If your church members can't picture their friends or relatives whom they want to invite coming to your church, then they are unlikely to refer it to them—*even* if it is very impactful to them personally. The sweet spot is when you have a great product in great packaging. We've talked about the packaging, but your Ministry is the real "product" inside it.

## HOW MINISTRY HAPPENS

A friend of mine says that he has a fourfold vision: people, people, people, and people. This has got to become true about your church. Even though we are building systems, you can't allow yourself to get lost in them or even really focus on them once they are up. Systems are really just ways that we initiate and facilitate people touching people. Most people are not going to hit a 10 on the Promoter Scale through great videos and coffee alone (especially since the church up the road probably has that too). But they will refer your church if they have made real and lasting friendships or received significant care. It's the long game that counts.

*If you have a video miscue you can laugh it off, but if you miscue with a life, you'll weep it off.*

Challenge yourself when you are talking about all of the functions of your church to talk about people, people, people. Talk about individual names as much as possible—positively of course. If God knows the number of hairs on each person's head in your congregation, how much more does He know each name, and each story, and care about each one? If you have a video miscue you can laugh it off, but if you miscue with a life, you'll weep it off.

The fundamental thing that you need to understand in order to build healthy and functioning ministry systems is the power of free will. **You cannot force people to grow or to hunger for the Lord.** If you try, you will create backlash which may appear in ways that you cannot expect. When I was younger and inexperienced, I would, from benevolent motives, jump in the middle of people's situations and try to push, pull or urge them forward in their lives. This was a recipe for disaster. I found out most people are where they are for deep reasons which have to be addressed *with their own initiative* before they can move forward.

I used to think of myself more like rescuer, but now I think more like gardener. If I create the right growing environment, the plants will grow. Paul describes this in 1 Corinthians 3:6. "I planted the seed, Apollos watered it, but God has been making it grow." It's our job to plant and water, but it is the Holy Spirit working with a person that brings growth. He sets the pace.

I have come to summarize it this way: "The Miracle is in the Pull." Or sometimes I say, you cannot push a string. If someone isn't ready for their miracle, you can't force it on them. When you take a closer look at the miracles of Jesus, you discover that in most cases, the person had to do something to activate their healing. From the woman who chased him down in the crowd (Luke 8:45) to the Canaanite woman who wouldn't take no for an answer (Matt 15:22-29) to the man who couldn't walk who was told to take up his mat (John 5:8), the miracle was activated by the action they took. Conversely, you may remember the story of Namaan, who almost missed his miracle because he refused to take the step of activation given to him (2 Kings 5). It's when someone is ready to pull, that things begin to happen.

The principle of the pull is equally observed in Jesus' personal outreach. He did not chase people down, but rather He continually invited them to follow. This has significant consequences for your ministry activities. You cannot make someone take steps they are not ready for. You should present an avenue for change but not force it because *the miracle is in the pull.* The church creates an environment where people can take action and gives them the inspiration to do so, praying for them the whole way through. But only when someone becomes hungry for the next step will anything significant happen.

How do you do this? Every nice fishing boat has a "live well," a place to put the fish once you catch them so that they stay alive until you can get them to shore. That's how your Sunday service operates – it's a place where people can stay until they are ready for the next step. You should invite them to go further down the Ministry and Growth pathways you've constructed but not expend energy trying to push them down the path.

In fact, I encourage you to think of all of your ministry vehicles that way. It's good to encourage and recruit, but at the end of the day, you need people to opt into the next step. Until they do, it's good for them to swim around in the live well until they are ready. The ministry system allows your community to come alongside those who are choosing to opt-in and help them. Encourage leaders with pastoral giftings to oversee these roles, they will flourish there..

## THE ASSOCIATE PASTOR

The first type of ministry and care that has to happen in any church is traditional, or what I would term "symbolic" ministry. This includes most of the functions traditionally associated with being a pastor including dedicating babies, doing weddings, funerals, hospital visits, and remembering key holidays. You can make your own list based on what is important in your community. Symbolic touches like these mean a lot to people even though they do not directly solve a particular problem. This is because people see them as holy moments, and the pastor as the mediator of the holy. Your presence for these moments can be a make-or-break moment for someone and their connection to your church.

At the same time, these can take a lot of time and are often not directly related to ministry or growth, so it's tempting to try and avoid them once you start down the church growth pathway. Instead, I recommend that you view them formally as part of Outreach because most of these kinds of activities give you an opportunity to touch people outside of the immediate sphere of your church. What better opportunity than a local wedding or funeral to put you in front of a large number of non-believers? If you do these well, you could see an influx of people who feel connected to you already.

One challenge you may find as you grow is that these kinds of activities can multiply yet be hard to offload to others, since people often want to be touched by *the Pastor*. This is the traditional reason for the emergence of the Associate Pastor. A good Associate Pastor is someone you trust that has a natural, personal pastoral touch, but not a strong need to be in charge of the church. When you can identify and hire someone like this, it's important to give them prominence on the platform or elsewhere so that these kinds of needs can flow to your Associate more naturally. The principle is that people usually connect with the leaders they hear from onstage.

The Associate Pastor role is at the core of the Ministry System. The Associate Pastor's role is found in most large successful churches because it fulfills an essential social function. They are often the hub of the community when it comes to greeting and care. Think of the Associate Pastor as the first point of contact, or triage nurse. When someone has a struggling marriage, where do they go? They will likely come to you first as the pastor, but if you have a well-established Associate, then they will find them next. It's ideal if you can place a pastorally oriented couple in this role, or if not, leverage another leader on your team to ensure that you have both a man and a woman who can field these requests.

The Associate Pastor needs to provide the safe friendly place where people can feel connected and receive spiritual direction, but they should not try meet everyone's needs personally. Instead, as the triage nurse, the job is to help those coming to find what they need through the resources of the church body. For most situations, they can and should refer them to Ministry groups or Growth groups most closely related to their needs. They will find a supportive community, helpful instruction, and other capable leaders here.

The Associate should have a shelf of trusted resources to help people accelerate their own journey. They can also refer and connect them directly with potential friends and mentors within the church who are best suited to walk alongside them. For difficult situations, the Associate Pastor should have at least one trusted professional counselor they can refer out to, and other referrals to specialized ministry such as Teen Challenge, etc.

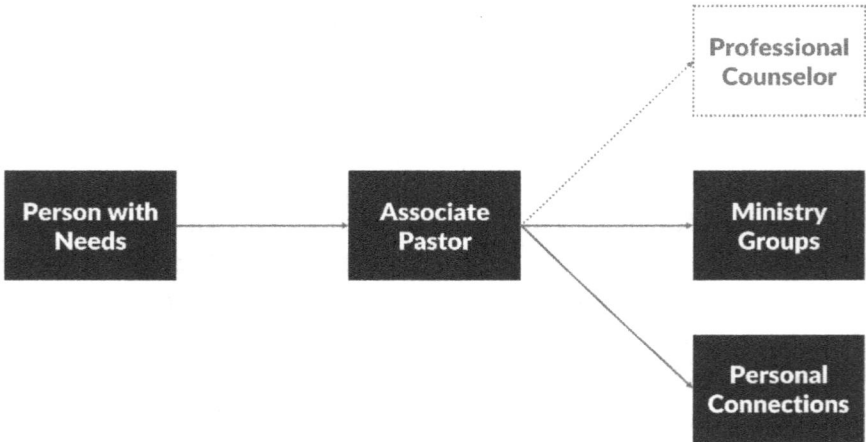

I cannot overstate the importance of the Associate role, not just to your church's ministry system, but to all of your systems working well. No matter how much you communicate, most people will never fully understand the brilliant architecture of your master plan of systems... but they can know to look for Pastor Steven when they come to church with their needs. When this triage role is being properly filled, the associate ensures that people will get their needs addressed, will not fall through the cracks because they don't know where to go, and also that they will not be overly invested with anyone in the church.

## MEETING BASIC NEEDS

A good Ministry system starts by meeting the kinds of challenges that everyone faces in life. These are the pieces you have to build first so that your triage nurse has a place to send the patients. The biggest categories are family and financial. From a ministry growth perspective, the good thing about these needs are that these are areas where people actually want to grow because they are feeling the pain of their current challenges! They are also areas where the church is seen as competent to provide that help.

Conversely, other areas that people need to grow in, such as leadership, personal responsibility, or spiritual hunger, are not obvious deficits people spot in themselves, so you have to create awareness of those before you can create a system to address them.

In fact, family and financially related ministries are often reasons that people seek church in the first place! People with any kind of church background know and believe that the church is a place where they can get help for their struggling marriage or wayward child. So this is a great opportunity to fulfill the expectations of the hurting world around you. These kinds of ministries provide just as much of an invisible front door as the website or the sign out front. For this reason alone, it's essential that every church have systems that help address core family needs. If you don't have them, you are missing out on huge growth opportunities.

**Family Ministry.** In the department of family, there are several main areas where people commonly want ministry and there are an abundance of great Christian tools. **Pre-marital** and newlywed ministry focuses on giving happy couples the right foundations and tools for a successful future. **Marriage ministry** helps give couples tools to improve their marriages or address challenges. Our church has several marriage groups which address different phases of marriage like the early years, "in the thick of it" years, and empty-nest years. **Parenting ministry** gives tools to help parents raise great children. If you are around long enough to reap the fruit, solidifying families can bless you in countless ways. There are also parenting related ministries like MOPS (Mothers of Preschoolers) which many churches do for both ministry and outreach purposes.

**Financial Ministry.** Financial issues are a major source of stress for many couples, and many people in our society live just on the edge or beyond their budget. Implementing a proven curriculum such as Dave Ramsey's *Financial Peace* can be a game-changer for couples as well as your church. A side benefit of a curriculum like this is that it also teaches people the importance of tithing. As people free up resources, they become happier and also more able to support your mission, by giving to the church.

In addition to these traditional ministries for families, you can also consider **Divorce Care** which can provide a unique door to reaching lost people as well as helping members of your congregation. I had a friend from high school reach out to me who was going through marital problems. He had no particular faith background, but I was able to recommend to him a Divorce Care group hosted by a local church. They gave him positive contact with believers that he had probably never had before. A similar ministry that can perform both ministry and outreach is **Grief Share.** This group focused on helping people deal with the loss of loved ones.

**Recovery Ministry.** You may also have a class of people who are facing fundamental life management issues stemming from a lack of character development, including addiction. While this was once a small part of our society, it is now a major segment of society. If your church is not equipped to handle people in these situations, they will either go away unchanged to find a church that can help them, or they will siphon away significant resources from the church body as you try to help them.

For this reason, I highly recommend **Celebrate Recovery**. It is a very well-developed and proven approach to dealing with people who have struggled with major life challenges. It's the perfect "live well" for people in that struggle. They will find friends and mentors, and will not solely rely on you for care. In addition, it can be an outstanding doorway into your church. People will find out about your church through Celebrate

Recovery's network. As they become stable, they may start their own groups and minister to people in other similar situations, and take pressure off of you.

One church I attended had such a large Celebrate Recovery ministry that it became a major wing of the church. Ultimately, they became a pillar in their community. I see this as complimentary to other freedom paths which you may also put in place depending on the needs in your community. My experience is that recovery from life-controlling issues needs a long-term structured approach to help people rebuild.

For those who are in more serious situations than a support group can handle, I suggest that you establish a relationship with Teen Challenge or another similar structured program where you can help them check in. Don't take on a project that is beyond your capacity and experience. It will siphon you and your congregation dry.

Having your church set up to help people in these kinds of situations goes a long way in giving valid and effective ministry avenues to people in difficult situations. As someone who spent several years of my life doing street ministry, and now as leader of a national prison ministry, I can say that a lot of ministry that people do is well-intentioned but not particularly effective—and sometimes not particularly needed.

For example, I vividly remember the leader of one Teen Challenge I visited who had grown tired of churches coming to mow the grass and do little projects for him. He told them bluntly, "I don't need your white guilt projects." On the other hand, he was eager for mentors who could commit to the hard work of walking alongside a man in recovery. Remember that doing things for people that they can't do for themselves helps them, but doing things they should do for themselves hurts them. If you haven't read it, you should read *When Helping Hurts* by Brian Fikkart. The best ministry is when churches empower people to rise, not when we give them stuff.

There are lots of other niche ministries that you can

explore and build as you gain capacity. Depression and anxiety are widespread issues, especially for women. Purity related groups are great as well, as long as you can keep them positive. Building a specialized group for these kinds of issues can be really transformative. Single moms face unique challenges that you can look at addressing. The same is true of parents with special needs kids, as well as adoptive and foster parents. Consider who you have coming to your church, and the gifts of your leaders, and what vessels of care seem right for your context. You can't and don't have to build Rome in a day.

### MINISTERING TO CHILDREN AND YOUTH

*Many adults who convert do so because their children's needs are being met through a church setting.*

Statistics tell us that most everyone who converts to Christianity does so before they are 25. Furthermore, many adults who convert do so because their children's needs are being met through a church setting. This means that if you do not have a vibrant ministry to young people, you are letting a part of the harvest pass you by. How can you engage this critical demographic?

For preschool and elementary age children, the best thing you can do is have a reliable, life-giving children's ministry during your Sunday service. Many parents of young children, especially in contemporary society, are simply desperate for a break from their children. They get so much ministry just from sitting with their spouse and thinking clearly for a few minutes. If you can create an environment where parents can bring their children and come to church together, they will often stay based on that fact alone.

For this reason, children's ministry is paramount. Since most young children are coming with their parents, the very best ministry to a child is for their parent to find Jesus and start to live differently. As it concerns the child's experience in children's church, making it safe and enjoyable is often enough.

We of course want God-centered messages and activities, but the testimonies of children whose hearts were touched in their formative years often report that it was the teacher or other factor beyond what they *did*, that transferred to them the love of God.

Mainstream youth ministry today tends to be focused on fun and field trips to attract students. This can lead to pastors hiring "the guy who never grew up" to be the youth leader, which then perpetuates the stereotype of youth group as a party. Instead of hiring the guy who never grew up, or a single unmarried college-age girl, it's better to look for a young couple that has a heart to heavily invest in youth and connects well with them. Other young people who have graduated from high school but want to be involved as mentors can help as co-leaders. This structure will help you build a culture of purity, as well as give your students role models they can look up to.

I want to also share a hard-learned lesson here as well. I grew up in liberal Presbyterian church, and then nearly died in an accident, which caused me to become incredibly hungry for God and eventually encounter the Holy Spirit. This led me to a skewed view of how young people respond to the Holy Spirit. I thought it was something awesome that people were keeping me away from, but most kids who are raised around the Holy Spirit don't have that same perception.

My kids have been raised around prophets and high level prophetic ministry, and while it has definitely impressed them at times, what has impacted them most are moments when I'm just being a good dad, or when we take a car ride and talk about God over ice cream. In Spirit-filled circles, we say things like "there is no junior Holy Spirit" meaning that anything adults do we should focus on releasing to the youth and that this will be the decisive factor in their growth. While children need the Holy Spirit, they need to be introduced to Him at the pace of their own hunger and willingness in the context of all of the other healthy aspects of life. It's amazing when a child of 9 can prophesy in detail, but it's more amazing when that child grows up to walk with the Lord.

The main reason why kids come to youth group is to see their friends, but that's not a bad thing. If you build culture around Jesus, this social drive can be used for good. The goal should be to build a youth culture that is focused on passion for and surrender to Jesus, and to raise up students to be leaders—to have Outreach, Growth, Ministry, and Leadership within their sphere just like the adult church.

For this reason, it can help to think of youth group like a church plant all of its own. You do many of the same kinds of things you would do to plant an adult church. You want to build a **critical mass** of students so that they will want to be there to see each other each week. You can do this through fun, invitational kinds of **events** designed to attract, or field trips that build momentum.

About six times a year, our church's youth group holds a party instead of a service and incentivizes students to bring new friends. They also will take small teams to attend each other's school sports events, dance recitals, or other activities where support and outreach can occur. There are games and contests on a somewhat regular basis because some amount of fun needs to be a part of any youth group experience. But fun does not have to be the dominant theme. At the core, youth group should be seen as a service to help young people encounter Jesus—just like on Sundays.

As for the youth group meeting itself, the ideal is to build toward a youth-driven service. We started ministering to youth, but when some youth arose who were able to do the ministry themselves, everything changed. Instead of going to a prayer meeting, they were leading prayer. Instead of hearing another message from an adult, they were cheering their friends on. The more youth driven you can build, the more momentum you will have.

The service runs a bit like a week of church in a box: there is first with worship in a large group setting, then corporate prayer, a message, and finally a time of small group discipleship. Each meeting starts off with a "pre-party" for the first half hour when students are arriving. There are sodas, music, and some fun things to do while everyone is seeing their friends. Then comes a 30-minute worship set, mostly led by young people, with prayer at the end, or praying the Scriptures. This helps everyone connect, but leads them into uniting around Jesus.

On this note, we have found that people relate to and learn most quickly from their peers, and youth do especially. When you have your students lead worship, pray on the mic, or speak from the platform, you build them into leaders. You also provide role models to the less mature youth around them. It sets the tone that God is the main thing.

We have also found that junior and high school students benefit from having leaders who are solid young adults, college or just post-college age. The leaders themselves benefit too, because mentoring youth helps them avoid the spiritual wasteland that can easily occur between high school and marriage. They develop spiritually and emotionally by supporting the youth group, and the youth get role models they can look up to and connect with because they are only one phase of life ahead. It's a win-win.

After worship and a message, our students break into small groups by age and gender. Small group time focuses on debriefing the message and enables discipleship to happen because they can talk about applying the message to what they're really going through. During this time, remember your goal is to raise up leaders among the youth, so you want to sow into those kids who can become role models, and also into those who might be on the fringes but for whom a little attention can be life-changing. Many students are at youth group specifically because they don't fit elsewhere or aren't getting what they need at home. If they can find a home in a community centered on Jesus, their lives can be different forever.

Lastly, within the church at large, don't compartmentalize youth. Find ways to engage them as part of the Sunday service and any other regular services you have throughout the week. Perhaps one of the best parts of my church-planting life has been that my children have become co-owners of our church because they have roles on Sunday just like we do. There is no youth service which takes them out of the adult experience. They are welcomed in the adult worship service, and with adults serving on service teams in the facility. When our children first started serving, they were late elementary and middle school age and served in Children's ministry. Later most of them served at the Production booth, and now on Worship team and Creative teams. It's not my church that I take them to, it's their church.

## OTHER DEMOGRAPHIC-BASED MINISTRIES

You want groups to help people grow, and for this reason, every ministry activity you create should have a clear input and output. The input is the target audience for the activity, and the output is the change that results from their participation.

If you do not consider input and output, you will naturally build things that are stagnant in nature. Demographically defined ministries run this risk, meaning "Men," "Women," and "Young Adults" describes the people we want to reach, but not what we hope to have happen. Therefore, while it is definitely appropriate for some kinds of ministry to be done in age or gender-segregated ways, I recommend not overemphasizing the demographic itself.

Remember, any community that is not intentionally turned outwards naturally turns inward, and demographically defined ministry encourages a tendency encourage connecting people for the sake of connection. Therefore, rather than define these ministries by their demographics, the ideal is to define them by objectives. The primary fellowship of the disciples happened while they were on mission.

For example, women in general have a strong desire to gather and connect. This God-given desire is essential for the functioning of every healthy community that has ever existed on planet. The key is for you to harness this energy in a way that reaches outwards, not only inwards. If you are going to hold a women's event, for example, you need to think about who you are going to attract, and what they are going to do as a result. Is this an outreach? It is a launch activity? Is it to deeper, grow, or heal something in some way? If you can't answer that question, you probably shouldn't hold the event.

Conversely, men do not generally have the same strong desire to connect, i.e. just *because* they are men. Many men simply want to achieve, or be a successful father/husband. Men tend to be project-oriented and are motivated by access to senior leader. The strongest communities of men will therefore be built in places where they are on mission together.

This means that if you a male senior pastor, you need to see yourself be the chief men's minister even if you have an official men's minister. Consider making your own small group where men who want to take the next step with God or the church can connect with you. Look for ways that the men of the church can be deployed and grow around projects, including leadership in the church, activities associated with the facility, service projects in the community, and groups that enhance their career and family life goals.

Young Adults (approximately 18-25 year olds) can be a particularly challenging demographic to serve and connect with unless you are a very youth-oriented church. Young Adults often disappear into a spiritual abyss during these years, or leave and go to a church geared toward them. Many large churches have a "singles" ministry, but as a friend of mine once commented, "It's the only part of the church that is created around something most people *don't* want to be…" i.e. "single." Singles ministry ends up having the connotation that it is supposed to be a place to meet your spouse, or date, and then leave.

So while I don't personally recommend a "singles" ministry, a vibrant church is one that fosters a marriage-positive culture. It is important to celebrate family at every stage, and to be positive about young couples who find each other at your church. Sometimes church leaders will have the tendency to either get so aggressive about a purity culture that they stifle the natural mutual discovery process that happens through dating, or will get so involved in the process that people's lifelong decisions get enmeshed with the dynamics of the church or leaders. What you can and should do is set the tone of purity at the leadership level, and create groups which will help young people who want to marry get there. Our church once ran a "future husbands club" where a married man gave hard truths to the guys, and not only was it the most popular men's group we ever did, it produced the intended result.

Overall our approach to growing youth and young adults is not to cordon them off to the side of the church as "youth" or "singles," but to include and feature them in as many ways as possible including time on stage and leadership roles. Pinpoint mature young people who can lead groups within your Growth, Ministry and Outreach systems that are youthful in nature. We can be a church of all generations if we are intentional to welcome each other.

### MINISTRY EVENTS

The encounter-based Sunday service is an event that you and the team have built to create encounter and invite them to go deeper. The Sunday service is specifically designed to help lead people into encountering Jesus and from that to ministry or growth, but the Sunday event is not the only event that benefits your church. Anything you want to build can be launched with an event because events create momentum. In fact, an event is how you launch the church itself, so it only makes sense that events are critical for launching other activities – which can then be harnessed in small groups.

You can easily see this principle in operation by observing events like fundraisers and evangelism crusades. The purpose of these events is to gather and surface those who are ready to take the next step, but that number is always much smaller than the number of people at the event. This makes a small group the most logical way to follow through on the energy created in the event.

Events operate like a spring – you put in a lot of energy to load them up, and then when you hold the event, a lot of energy is released which must be capitalized on to make the event worthwhile. If you decide to hold events for men or women, they should be directly tied to outreach, growth, or ministry objectives, and then instrumented to capitalize on the momentum that comes from them.

Anything you want to grow, you can and should grow with an event. For example, because parenting and marriage needs are widespread throughout any congregation, seminar-style events which are attractional can check many boxes – attracting, informing and connecting. Similarly, if you want a vibrant ministry targeting the needs of women in your church, you can hold a women's event as a springboard. These springboards become fresh on-ramps to other activities in the growth and ministry system, which are often delivered in a small group format.

Creating ministry groups allows you to have a "live well" for the different kinds of needs that come to your desk as pastor. Instead of taking on challenging problems, you can give people the opportunity to feed themselves through various ministry groups. The beauty of having ministry groups is that people "opt in" for care. Remember that "miracle is in the pull" – it is their decision to take a step which starts to activate transformation. I have learned to apply the "matching grant" philosophy to ministry – I will do as much for you as you are willing to do for you, but not more. This helps screen out the difference between those who really need help and those who could siphon you dry.

While many churches look a small groups as their own thing, I prefer to look at small groups as a delivery format. Important aspects of Outreach, Ministry and Growth can all be met through a healthy small group format, but small groups are just the format, not their own system. Each of these systems needs its own leader focused on the unique needs of that system.

By having an Outreach director, a Growth director and a Ministry director, you'll get much more focus on the target. An ideal Outreach director, for example, would be a person with an evangelistic flare who can oversee outreach groups, events, and awareness building with the singular focus of contacting the lost. When run generic "small groups" the specific objectives of the systems get lost—along with your potential impact and growth.

The systems are defined by the unique objectives they are trying to fulfill. You may run Growth groups as a class or as a small group. Much of what you put in the Growth track can be delivered in small group format to promote interactivity and personal growth. For example, a foundations class would be a great formatted as a small group, as would Freedom. Ministry because it permits a smaller, private space to provide extended care. This would also allow people in similar situations in life to meet potential new friends.

Because events are logical launch points, and groups are logical catch points, I am a big fan of running groups on a semester-system. While some have that small groups take the place of church events, I strongly believe that the two should work together. Events are ideal launching pads into small group based ministry. Semesters provide places during the year where you can launch groups through events. You put a lot of energy into these launch times, which encourages people to join the places they will receive deeper ministry and care. If you're on a semester, they know that the commitment is well-defined so they can exit when they are done. Similarly, for leaders who may have grace in certain seasons but cannot lead groups all the time. Perpetual programs or groups also become tight knit over time and have the problem of being awkward for newcomers to join and uncomfortable for them to leave.

Furthermore, because of the school calendar and the seasons, most people's life outside of church is logically structured into Fall, and Spring; some have Winter or Summer semesters that can be leveraged too. It is both easy and logical to use this natural structure as you implement small groups in your church. The group runs for the length of the semester and then can easily be disbanded or renewed. This provides easy on and off ramps for people, which is an incredibly important thing for growth.

## TYPES OF SMALL GROUP SYSTEMS

Since the explosion of Dr. Cho's church in South Korea, there have been numerous attempts to incarnate his cell group model with varying degrees of success. The idea of the cell group was a self-replicating group of believers – a house church within the larger church body that was specifically designed and expected to grow and divide just like a cell. This model seems to work best in cultural conditions that are very favorable to the spread of Christianity. It facilitates very rapid expansion of the faith and growth of a church.

However, in places like the contemporary United States or Europe, growing and replicating a cell is a small miracle in itself, because it means that many people are finding salvation rapidly – something that is very difficult when most people have a long way to move on the Engel Scale. Some successful large churches in the US have used the concept of a "micro-church" led by trusted leaders, to funnel people who want deeper community, but it's different than a replicating cell, it's a community of friends inside of the larger body.

To be honest, some of those systems are only really needed or relevant if you are running a church with many thousands of people. The overall goal of the encounter-based church is not to become that big, and launch many campuses but to raise up and support leaders who launch their own churches once you are beyond a few thousand. This is because there is a ceiling on how many people a single pastor can truly lead, and that same ceiling holds back developing leaders from launching their own works.

The idea of a small group is similar but not identical to either a cell or a micro-church. It is a group of believers of up to 20 who are focused around a specific topic – not around general fellowship or self-replication. Small groups have the beautiful benefit of allowing for processing and interactivity which is a huge part of learning and growth. At Prison Fellowship where I work, we emphasize the importance of small groups in our prison programs for exactly this reason.

One of the most successful implementations of small groups in America so far has been the "market-based" small group. In the market-based system, people create small groups based on their own interests, and gather people of like mind. The advantage of the market concept is that it channels free-market forces in the creation process. The idea is that, in any given season, people typically know better what they want and need than centralized planners do.

Having people lead their own startups offloads a lot of work that would normally become a big church project for some individual on staff. By equipping people to do small groups, you can resolve the age-old problem of people expecting you to build every ministry they want, the way they want it. Every pastor is very familiar with the person who tells them all about what the church should be doing. The "everything is a small group" model gives the ready-made answer to this problem by encouraging someone to be their own solution. If you execute this strategy well, you can actually build an entrepreneurial ecosystem where trusted people are supported to pilot and grow ministries.

On the other hand, while there are significant advantages to free market small groups, there are also disadvantages. In a true free market, people are more likely to do things they want, rather than things they need—they are more likely for example, to start another Bible study for their friends than an outreach. Also, random people may end up nominating themselves as leaders, which can cause its own set of issues.

For these reasons, I believe that small groups are best as a "managed market" where leaders you trust are empowered to meet the felt-needs of the congregation or chartered to lead ministry endeavors. Remember, your goal is to build components which take people on a journey of maturity.

# The Leadership System

## THE COMMISSION

The final phase of discipleship is leadership. A fully mature disciple of Jesus has the capability to lead others toward the Lord, and to drive change in the systems of the world around them. The Bible is written around the activities of leaders. They are the Daniels, the Josephs, the Davids, the Peters and Pauls. Not everyone reaches this phase of development or becomes fully mature in it, but to be healthy and fulfilling its mission, a church must be producing leaders.

This is, in fact, the reason why the dedicated ministry staff exist:

> Christ himself gave the apostles, the prophets, the evangelists, the pastors and teachers, **to equip his people for works of service** (Eph 4:11-12a)

Our mission is to build up the Body of Christ and release them into their callings to change the world. The church is an outpost of heaven where we rescue the captives and send them back into battle to bring light to the world.

*Our mission is to build up the Body of Christ and release them into their callings to change the world.*

We must be careful not to define success in terms of things that only happen inside the church. This would be like if all military successes were defined as things that happened on the base or in the field hospital. Our true success comes as we are impacting the world around us. It's reaching the lost but it's also transforming the world's systems to reflect God's values.

When the salt loses its savor, the end result is that we are thrown out and trampled by men (Matt. 5:13). The current secularization of the West is partly a result of our taking too narrow of a view of what matters. Therefore, the leaders that we are looking to build, equip, and celebrate exist across the full spectrum of life. The church can't do this all on its own, but it's our responsibility to create a culture where this is normal.

## WHO IS FOLLOWING YOU?

To have a leadership pipeline in your church, you must first be the leader of your church. I know this may sound axiomatic, but many pastors, especially in established churches, are effectually the chief servant of the church. In order for your church to move forward, you must be established as the leader. You must behave like someone who is to be followed, as opposed to someone who is following.

For this reason, I consider leadership to be the chief competency of a pastor. A great pastor must be a good communicator, have a good personal touch, and live a solid life. But his most important quality is inspiring people to follow him, and then managing those relationships well.

Fundamentally, a church is a volunteer organization. While it has leadership and a paid staff, the church only exists based on a desire of people to spend their free time and resources there. This makes it different from a business or governmental entity. People have to want to come on the journey in order for the organization to succeed. This means your organization will not go anywhere until people are following you. Your strength as a leader is directly tied to who is following you. It is important that you build up this leader-follower relationship, and then rely on those who are following.

Think of three categories of relationships: ministry, friends, and followers. Many leaders with a great pastoral gift mistake ministry or friend relationships for followers. Ministry is when you are coming alongside someone, adapting yourself in ways that create relationship so they will be open to truth. This is often what we think of when we think of "pastoring" someone. It is showing special care for their life by going the extra mile. I have helped many people in this mode of relationship, (this is what my forthcoming book *The Emmaus Road* is about), but I have also learned not to confuse pastoral care with leadership. Those I'm pastoring are generally not following me, they are receiving ministry from me.

Similarly, friends are those who like you and enjoy your company. No one is following anyone. My friend appreciates something about who I am, and I in turn appreciate things about them. There is parity which means often a true mutual friendship does not work well in a leadership context. If you try to lead your friends suddenly, you can lose them.

Instead, in order to build a church, you need to build on your followers: those who chose to do what you are doing because they respect you and your relationship with God. There is a fundamental disparity in this kind of relationship that makes it work. Jesus did not chase His followers – He invited them to follow Him. That is how you know who you can build on. Who is following whom? If you have to chase someone down, it's more of a ministry relationship, not one you can build on.

Structurally speaking, I believe the relationship between a leader and their followers can be expressed in terms of goals. When the relationship is healthy, it is because the goals of the person and the goals of the organization are aligned. This means that both are headed in the same direction and have the internal desire to do so. When this alignment exists, followers are following leaders, and there is mutual benefit. When this tilts out of balance, you either have heavy-handed leadership or no leadership at all.

If a leader has too much power, the tendency is to have heavy-handed or exploitative leadership, where people are serving the goals of the church with limited benefit or alignment to their own personal goals. We're all familiar with this danger. It leads to servitude and burnout of volunteers and staff. We are less familiar with the dangers of the opposite extreme, where the leader is not well established, and are actually being led from behind. The church is not following the leader but individuals are trying to achieve their own personal goals through the church. This leads to pastor burnout. Neither of these is healthy.

I had a teacher once who strongly believed in equality of leadership, that the table should be round, and everyone should have a voice. After putting this theory into practice a few times, he concluded that, "When there is no leader, whoever does not agree is the leader." Coming from someone of his convictions, this statement stuck with me. If there is no real leader, you aren't going anywhere. God's plan for history was not built by consensus, but was to call and equip individuals to lead in a direction that others would follow. Paul said, "Follow me as I follow Christ." (1 Cor. 11:1).

*The way you carry yourself will either cue friends, followers, or ministry.* My simple definition of a follower is someone who takes direction from you. The way you carry yourself will either cue friends, followers, or ministry. It's good for you to express interest by reaching out to people, but if you start to chase them down, just realize you are now the follower. You are entering into a ministry relationship, not a leadership relationship. Likewise, if you are very transparent about your life with someone, you are cueing friendship. It's not that there is no room for transparency with followers, you just need to realize that there are healthy limits. Leaders are focused toward a goal and are continually inviting others to participate in that goal. "Come follow me," Jesus said. He knew where He was going and invited them to come along.

## LEADING IN A CHURCH STRUCTURE

Leadership is at the core of everything else you will do as a church. If you have leadership problems, you are capped out no matter what else you are doing right. A pastor has a very unique and challenging leadership function because he oversees a group of people that are paying him. This is quite different from most other leadership contexts!

When I was a manager at IBM, I could expect people to follow me because they were paid to do so. The culture of a corporation makes clear that if you are not well-aligned, you will be not be on the team much longer. Furthermore, in secular work, people leave their passions at home and come to a relatively neutral space where completing the work is all that matters.

A church is almost exactly the opposite. People are coming to participate in something that they deeply care about and are in most cases financially contributing to. Their friends and family are there. You cannot fire them if they misbehave – in fact, they may even be able to fire you. Furthermore, as pastor, you are expected to be a perfectly grace-filled role model in all circumstances. Finally, although being a pastor is incredibly difficult, it is one of those jobs that almost everyone imagines they could do! People are ready to give you all kinds of advice and put expectations on you that no one could possibly fulfill, because things look quite a bit easier on their side of the fence.

These dynamics make you and the entire organization vulnerable to great dramas. Of course, if you have been a pastor for any length of time, you already know all of this, but the question remains, how to deal with it?

Having spent some time in politics, I have come to believe that the closest similar kind of leadership role to a pastor is a politician. I am not making an ethical comparison here, but rather one of structure. Politicians have the same structural challenges that pastors do – their constituents put them there to lead, but also to serve. People expect strength but also customer service. It's a very tough role.

One way to look at this is through the lens of a "personal brand." What do people think when they hear your name? The more powerful your brand is, the more successful you will be as a leader. This means having good public relations skills.

Some people, when they realize the power of perception, make this a substitute for a living an active relationship with Jesus. I'm not suggesting that even a bit. Nothing of spiritual significance will happen at all if you are not close to Jesus. What I am pointing out is that when we are only focused vertically, it can cause us to ignore and be unaware of the way people perceive us and how much influence it has over their willingness to follow. When you make careless statements or fail to do the kinds of things that are socially and reasonably expected of you, you undermine your credibility as a leader. Conversely, when you identify with your constituents, they identify with you. Paul even shaved his head as part of a PR campaign in Acts 18:18.

The power of your brand and your organizational power are nearly identical. Perception becomes reality. In the 21st century, your brand extends beyond your physical personal to your social media as well. You are a role model, and what people see you do there will cue them in big ways not just about who you are, but about how they should act.

Another way to put this is, you live in a fishbowl. As long as you know that and attune correctly, this can work for you rather than against you. Just like a politician, you must avoid making controversial public statements, while highlighting the positive things going on in your life and church all the time. This is more than just maintaining a positive image – it's discipleship. When you have a great time of worship with your family, for example, and you share it online, you're not bragging, you're being a role model. People will be thinking about what they saw and how to emulate your life. So leverage the power of social media as a discipleship and leadership-building tool.

If, however, people perceive you as having been un-Christlike in the way you handled a conflict, it won't matter if you were right, what will matter is the way it affected how they saw you. You want to maintain grace and poise in a conflict because it will cover mistakes.

Over time, as you become more trusted and more successful as a leader, you have more power to lead the organization where you want to go. This relational structure is also why ceremonial acts are so important for pastors. Everyone imagines themselves as personally close to the pastor, regardless of how close they are in fact. A successful pastor builds and maintains that image.

Chuck Colson, the founder of Prison Fellowship, where I currently am, was a master at this. Whenever I travel the country, it is incredibly common for me to hear someone say, "I was very close to Chuck," or "Chuck was my mentor." After a while I realized that Chuck could not have personally been close to or mentored hundreds of people! He simply knew how to give the right kinds of personal touches that helped people feel close to him. He even had a bodyguard who had an encyclopedic memory of someone's connection to the organization or their giving history, who would help Chuck in sticky situations. A good pastor should master how to keep people feeling close.

> *Your personal touch has power to comfort, to connect, and to inspire: use it.*

Your personal touch has power to comfort, to connect, and to inspire: use it. The old kings of England realized this, which is why they traveled the country, touching the sick, and reinforcing the folk belief that the touch of the King would heal them. Whether or not anyone was ever healed in this way, I don't know, but what I can say is that the King touching the sick brought the people a great sense of personal connection to him, which increased his authority.

Of course, I don't advise you to promote the belief that only you can heal the sick, but realize that in your role you have many special opportunities that you should embrace. As mentioned, this includes baptisms, baby dedications, weddings, hospital visits, and greeting people after service. These are opportunities, not burdens. As you get to a much larger size, and you have a trusted right-hand person that everyone recognizes, you may be able to pass some of these things along, but when you're small, do them because it builds the church.

The way you live and model helps create culture, and culture is one of the most powerful elements of leadership. Many things are caught much more than they are taught. Perhaps the biggest thing I've learned from my time as a leader at my church is the power of positivity. Our pastor makes a point to stay positive as much as possible and expects the same from the staff. This creates a culture around him of uplifting energy. For people who have been in deep, intense ministry this can feel a bit inauthentic at first. But I have watched as it has done wonders for us over time.

When you're doing ministry with challenging people or just facing your own life circumstances, it's easy to see the glass half empty, even unintentionally, and focus on the negative. This can color your life in ways that you don't even see. A positivity model expected by the pastor creates a culture, though, where you get used to seeing the best about yourself, about others, and your life circumstances. I've learned to smile more and have seen others get a serious life upgrade just by being around people who practice this kind of positive culture.

## IDENTIFYING LEADERS

As a pastor, once your leadership is established, you will be the most powerful person in that organization. That sometimes leads to the problem of people cuddling up to you because they want something – usually ministry opportunity but sometimes just your association or validation on their life. This can be confusing the first time it happens to you. Unless you've been in a position where you are accustomed to it, it's easy to mistake friendliness for true friendship. People need to earn their positions of trust and authority around you. It is unwise to give away any important position of leadership quickly.

This is not simply from skepticism about the character of others, but because all people need to go through the process of growth and shaping. Jesus says it plainly, "Whoever can be trusted with very little can also be trusted with much" (Luke 16:10). I believe this is an inviolable law of leadership. If you trust someone with much who has not yet been faithful with little, you can damage their character and your relationship with them. They can end up over their heads in responsibilities which they cannot succeed at, or potentially develop an inflated attitude about themselves. Promote progressively so that you have the opportunity first to shape whatever needs shaping.

On the other hand, if you do not reward the one who has been faithful with little by giving them more, you will drive them to find a different house to serve. When you see someone who begins to give indications that they are following, the first step is to give them something small to do and begin the process of growth. For example, the person who is faithful to clean the bathroom may have capacity to lead the facilities team, and in that capacity you may be able to coach them until they can lead on the platform. Each opportunity is a character building and testing step. Some people will be eager to rise, and some people will simply want to be a blessing through service. Knowing who is who can help you sort out how hard to lean on them and what opportunities to give.

Additionally, the process of sorting out who is following you and who is not takes some time—more time than you'd think. Some who appear to be supportive at first may not be, and some who seem not to be leaders at all may rise to the challenge. Some who appear "all-in" may grow disenchanted and move on, while those who were peripheral at first become believers in what you're doing and more capable.

One famous ministry leader says that he doesn't know if you are really a follower until he has given you a direction you don't like three times and you have done it. While I don't believe in intentionally putting people to the test, it is true that in difficult situations true character and motivations are revealed. You need to make sure that the people you put in positions of influence are willing to take direction from you, or when difficulty does arise, so will dissention. As time passes you will have the opportunity to observe their faithfulness and get a sense of their motivations. You have to trust God through this process and allow people to demonstrate their character over time. And the truth is that life is not static. People need time to self-sort their desires out which change as time goes on. People have life changes that move them on. People grow in capacity or respond to different needs that emerge which they can fill, as time passes.

Although it is tempting, it's unwise to put people into places of leadership quickly because of their experience, skill, or capacity. Rather, look for those who demonstrate the character of Jesus and are following you. You want people who come with a heart of service, not seeking position. You will be surprised by God if you partner with Him to sort out who is who!

When you read the book of Esther, it's easy to wonder how King Xerxes could have allowed Haman, who clearly wanted his throne, to have so much power. However, clearly Haman treated Xerxes one way, and those beneath and around him another way. With the power he had, Haman probably also controlled a lot of the information flowing up to Xerxes as well. That made it very difficult for Xerxes to discern who Haman really was. Fortunately for Xerxes, God exposed Haman before Haman did greater damage to his kingdom. Mordecai, on the other hand, was an unknown official barely on the radar of the king at all. He had actually saved the king's life and raised a girl with character enough to be his wife. God promoted him because his heart and capacity lined up with the king's needs.

This is a major challenge of leadership – I often liken it to the view from the top of a mountain. From the top of a mountain it is easy to see for long distances, but very difficult to see the mountain below. Since you are standing on it, a great deal of the mountain is obscured by the mountain itself. At the top of a leadership structure, what is really going on below you can be difficult to see because it is obscured by those in your immediate circle and the way they choose to present information to you. This is true even with loyal followers. Becoming aware of this and looking carefully for indicators that can help you see more can help you find Mordecai's and avoid Haman's.

Another challenge of leadership development is how direct to be with someone about what they need to do in order to rise farther. If you are direct with them right out of the gate, you may run them off before they have a chance to grow organically through serving. You can also create blowback unnecessarily. On the other hand, if you do not make clear to them what the path is, then they can exist in a kind of limbo state wondering if there is something wrong with them, which has nothing to do with what is holding them back.

I believe Jesus took a middle approach. He did not tell the disciples everything up front, but He always made clear to them what their path was. He was direct with them in response to their questions but did not correct everything all at once. For you to have positive collaboration, everyone always needs to know what their next step toward their own goal is. Remember the miracle is in the pull. As we work and pull, we are transformed.

Your church and your leaders grow together. When you are small, you may have many roles covered by the same person, and as you grow, you will be able to create more and more specialization. Over time, you'll have leaders of leaders. The role a person plays should change over time as they grow and as the church itself grows. When you have someone who is serving well, leading with excellence and aligned to you, you should adapt roles to fit who they are so they can grow into their full potential. Don't keep your top performers stuck in a role that is not their power-alley.

When you step back and look at your entire church and all the systems, you'll see all the people who serve and minister in your systems are also in your leadership pipeline. They are being trained, and as they are, you are raising them up. You can see how this process over time will lead you to strong and supportive teams. It will also create significant leadership capacity within your teams. As you build the culture of leadership, you are doing more than building your church, you are giving people capacity that will make them successful in whatever paths they take in the rest of life as well.

## LEADERSHIP MEETINGS

Meetings are at the core of the leadership system, and just like every other system in the church, you want to make sure that your leadership meetings are accomplishing their purpose: moving the church forward and developing your leaders. When you are meeting too frequently, you are chewing up valuable energy talking to each other rather than doing. When you are not meeting enough, people fall out of sync and connection. Your core team needs to meet every week in addition to your other informal interactions with them. Many of your wider circles of volunteer leadership can meet monthly.

Likewise, when meetings go too long, that often means you are not using the time wisely. This may be because topics which do not need to be discussed in the full group are taking over, or there may be arguments or discussions with no clear leadership. A great meeting always has a leader and a set of objectives. A good meeting has healthy discussion too, but it isn't helpful to have discussion devolve into debate or inaction.

Your leadership meeting is probably the most powerful time of discipleship you have during the week because it is when you are using your power as leader to shape what and how people do things. It's easy for meetings to become all about small operational problems, but if you want to lead an encounter-based church, it is essential that you make them first about Jesus, second about people, and last about operations.

This is how you communicate what is important. By making Jesus important, you welcome Him to your service and encourage your staff to make Him first priority in how they lead. By making people important, you grow the church by being faithful with those God sends. You can always talk offline about operations, but you don't want Jesus to go offline. Remember that all of the work you are doing is to change people's lives. You worked incredibly hard to bring them there, and Jesus worked even harder to save them. Give those lives the spotlight at your meetings, and put operations into proper place.

For these reasons, as a senior leader at Prison Fellowship, I literally never start a meeting without prayer. I am setting the tone that Jesus is the one who we want to really be leading the meeting, and that everything successful we could possibly do comes from our connection to Him. Sometimes I close in prayer of blessing over the staff, or even over their personal issues. Jesus is our source of connection, unity, and wisdom. We must "in all our ways acknowledge Him." (Prov 3:6)

### THE RIVER OF LEADERS

The end result of the encounter-based church is for a river of leaders to flow from your church. If your church is continually growing, and you are making room for strong leaders around you, then some of the leaders will be on your team, but if you are successful, many of them won't be. They will start churches related to yours, or ministries related to yours, or have Kingdom-oriented roles that flow in and out of church.

It's therefore important that we build in such a way that emerging leaders around us can grow. In a large church it can be hard for people to emerge because there is no room, or they can't connect to the pastor to have room made for them. This leads to a process of burn-out and churn-out where in order for someone to grow to the next level, they have to leave you. The sad irony of this, is that many of those who were themselves churned out because there was not room for them on the platform, then go on to replicate this system of building platforms where there is no room.

I believe the antidote for this cycle is what has been called the *culture of honor*. The end goal of the encounter-based church is not to build and release people. We do this by honoring and investing in the gifts within them. This means taking risks and creating opportunities for them to flourish, and showing them pathways to get from where they are to where they could be.

What you want is a pipeline of leaders who are attached to you, not a trail of potential leaders who left with unrealized potential. You want many sons instead of servants. For this reason, if your church becomes too big for a single campus, I believe the ideal process is that of launching a daughter church, rather than another campus. I don't know what the social limits of the encounter-based church is, but I believe the ideal church size is in the low thousands. If you get to that level and are thriving, you should have sons in the house who are ready to go and build with your full support.

### THE KINGDOM-MINDED LEADER

My life as a bi-vocational minister has given me a unique view of church life – both from the side of the attendee, and from the side of a pastor. It's hard to imagine two more different viewpoints of the church experience.

There are almost two different languages, and it is hard to bridge the gap. Attendees rarely have any understanding of the unique pressures on a pastor. To many of them it looks like a job with flexible hours, no boss, no deadlines, and the chance to be paid to talk and counsel others. They don't understand all the problems and temptations that come with being a pastor including the adulation and the pressure to be perfect all the time. A pastor doesn't have enough time for everything, but is responsible for everything, must please everyone, and do it all before God. Perhaps the biggest gap is that until you have lived through life as a senior leader, you simply don't know what it's like to be attacked by someone in the congregation for only trying to help them, and then to have members of your team take their side. These kinds of enormous pressures on a pastor make it a lonely road.

On the other hand, pastors who have spent little time in the marketplace often have a limited understanding of the pressures, problems, and needs of the average churchgoer. They can create expectations of doing a much higher amount of church and spiritual activity than is realistic for a busy working person or family. They may have a one-dimensional view of Christianity, seeing everything through the lens of church instead of realizing that attendees are usually committed to Jesus first, and their church as a distant second.

When you lead with Kingdom in mind, rather than just your church, people take note and will respect you for it. Remember that in the case of influencing the world for God, the pastor must have a vision for Christian leadership outside the walls of the church. That can be hard with all the systems and event planning going on, but it is an honor to affect the world for Jesus and see your people playing a part in that advance.

One part of that is giving a broader definition to what success looks like in the Kingdom. Most contemporary talk in church implicitly defines the Kingdom of God in a narrow way, as just being about evangelism and ministry. This has a lot of unfortunate side effects. One of them is that everyone who is really committed to the Lord is going to think that their goal is to become a paid minister.

If you define the Kingdom of God in larger terms, however, and train people to find ministry and excitement outside the walls, people will feel their horizons expand and be inspired to bring God into them. When large numbers of people become activated to change the world around them, it changes! In your congregation are the keys to the city! You will of course lose some capacity on your service teams, but most people will be able to contribute happily as volunteers or part-timers without pressing in to be full time staff. And ironically, your congregation will themselves start to fulfill the answers to some of the prayers you are praying for your city, nation, and world! We not only pray, but we act.

*In your congregation are the keys to the city!*

Think about this for a minute. Both China and Japan have had many waves of missionaries sent to reach their nations, yet China has had revival while Japan remains one of the most unreached nations in the world. What is the difference? Culture. Culture is the invisible set of values that determine whether or not people are open to the gospel or not. Culture is shaped over long periods of time by the people at the top of society in positions of influence. From the beginning of Bible history, God has put some of His people in these key positions to influence how the trajectory of a city or nation will go.

Consider an example closer to home. Why is evangelism generally harder in the U.S. Northeast than it is in a place like the Midwest? Having lived in several regions of the country, I can say that it's because the culture is different, and so is the history. Those in positions of power in New England for the last 100 years or more have been secular in their worldview, and pushed their secular values into schools and other institutions. When children who have been raised under this discipleship system grow up, they are predisposed against the Gospel.

Once you understand this, it is easy to understand why God raised up and profiled so many culture-makers in the Bible – Joseph, Moses, Daniel, Nehemiah, and Solomon come to mind as just a few examples. We simply cannot fulfill the Great Commission if we are not inspiring and training leaders to affect society at the highest levels.

Empowering Kingdom leaders who will bring God's ways into their own spheres of influence can be done in the church in many ways. First, by the way you talk from the pulpit. Do you celebrate people who are successful outside church, or only those who are inside? What you celebrate is what will be valued. By definition, church platforms are almost always filled only with ministers, which leads to the focus on church ministry.

In my first church in college, however, they brought in a wide array of successful business leaders to speak as well, which led to a different perception – that being successful in business was valued and so people wanted to do it. They also had professionals teach seminars about God's ways in fields like counseling and education. So more people began to think about a Biblical worldview of these jobs, and whether they might have a calling to pursue those.

God does amazing things through people's everyday jobs, so make sure to highlight and emphasize that when stories are told. We had a man get dramatically saved at our church because one of our staff was also working part-time at Starbucks. Which one of his jobs was really more important, in this case? At the Starbucks I frequent in the morning, something similar is going on. One of the young ladies is clearly a believer and has been influencing her co-workers in that direction. She is bringing the Kingdom right where she is.

Kingdom leaders do more than just witness, though. There are of course Kingdom politicians, educators, medical and security staff who change people's lives every day and imbue their fields with the ethics and counsel of God. Entrepreneurs like Truett Cathy, founder of Chick-fil-a, or the Green family, founders of Hobby Lobby, have had incredible Kingdom impact which almost cannot be measured.

First, through their giving and supporting major ministries around the country, but not just their giving. These businesses themselves are ministries. Have you ever paid attention to how Chick-fil-a employees behave? They are trained to think and act with Christian values regardless of what their faith is. Tim Scott, one of the only African-American senators, was discipled at a Chick-fil-a and gives this experience and the franchise owner credit for his success. For its part, Hobby Lobby has brought Christian décor into mainstream settings, making our culture a gentler place for everyone, not just people of faith.

Also consider the significant role that both of these companies have played in recent culture wars. It was only because of the strong moral values of Hobby Lobby and their willingness to stand up to governmental pressure, that organizations including churches do not have to pay for abortions.

These are just a few famous examples. The one who has a real estate business or construction crew in your church (and almost every church has these!) could have one of the most effective ministries in the church if you give them vision and equip them. One of my most powerful ministry friends was part of a crew of Christian guys. They would always have another non-believer with them, talking to him and discipling him as they worked on floors, tile, decks. Many men had their lives transformed this way. On the side, this man was a praying man and he used his gifts of prophecy and healing in amazing ways during our services.

*Look at your church as an incubator for Kingdom enterprise.*

Business is awesome ministry. When you see it as ministry in the marketplace, it can be fun. Until you see it that way, though, it can seem a long and difficult drudgery. Pastors can set people free when they give them this new view.

Look at your church as an incubator

for Kingdom enterprise. Help your people develop in their callings, not just in their ministry functions. God is the God of all of life. When your people see Him that way, they'll love you for it. There are many tactics you can use to help with this:

- **Selecting speakers** who are not from inside the ministry monastery. When people see God in action outside the church, it will give them vision and inspiration in the areas they are educated and gifted in.

- **Public celebration of successes** of those in your congregation. We shouldn't only talk about people when they are sick or dying. What about when they have major career and life successes?

- **Providing personal life coaching**, or empowering someone in your congregation to do so. As pastors we tend to look at someone's job as how they get paid, rather than as a way for them to flourish in life. Help them see God's career pathway for them and pray into it. Believe with them.

- **Connect the dots through networking groups**. People grow when they are in community with others who are likeminded. This can be through small groups with a marketplace focus, or by introducing people to others who could be mentors.

- **Welcome and partner with Kingdom-minded enterprises** and para-church ministries in your area. Doing this will have the side-effect of making your church the hub for ministry activity that extends beyond your reach as a local church. My organization of Prison Fellowship does this but so do myriads of Christian ministries and businesses.

- **Value professional skills and experience**. Marketplace people are often valued only when they tithe or are at the end of a 40-year career and can be put onto the Board of the church. People who are successful in the marketplace, however, have tremendous skills and wisdom that can bless the church in many ways long before then.

Each year, it becomes harder and harder to reach lost people in America because of our cultural decay. This decay is in large part a result of our failure to value and empower Christians to lead in *all* of life. Pastors have an important role in reversing this because of their power in leading and instructing the Body. The solution to our contemporary cultural woes is not simply great churches and reaching more lost individuals – it is raising up leaders who will help disciple institutions and bring God's ways, wisdom, and breakthroughs to society. As culture is more deeply touched by the presence of God, we will reach even more lost people. Remember, the Kingdom of God extends to all of life, not just salvation.

# Avoiding the Abyss

## Your Bulletproof Life

While the other five-fold functions have essential roles in setting up God's Kingdom, a God-ordained pastor is hosting an outpost of heaven on earth. For this reason, being a successful pastor requires that you be strong and well-rounded in many areas, especially the core areas of life.

Weaknesses you have will be magnified by the number and proximity of your followers, and the enemy will try any door he can find to halt your progress or corrupt the Body so that your ministry does harm rather than good. My wife and I were part of a church once where the Holy Spirit was active, but so was the spirit of control. People were being blessed *and* hurt at the same time. Unfortunately we have heard many stories with this kind of dynamic.

**Family.** To avoid this, you have to keep things pure from the top. To be a successful pastor, it is essential that you block and tackle really well. This means your marriage and children cannot be in the backseat of your life. They are not only your first ministry, but they are an essential part of your ministry success. My pastor has built his marriage and family so well that their simple presence and example ministers to our church every week. Even while he goes about his business, other couples are thinking about their example and how to be more like them.

**Devotional Life**. Right along with this is consistency in your walk with God. You don't need to have fireworks every day, but you do need to be steady and stable in your devotional life. Otherwise you will be like one who is tossed around by the wind (Eph. 4:14). A solid devotional life ensures that when things hit, you will have the reserves to pull from. If you get out of the Spirit, mistakes will be minimized because God's cover is on your life. God is always here to help us, but nothing is a greater daily vitamin and blessing to Him than our giving Him our hearts every day.

**Friends.** Pastors need friends. You can only have a certain depth of friendship with those who are following you, but you should still have peers and mentors who you can relate to and be vulnerable with locally and non-locally. In ministry we often find ourselves with other ministry-minded friends whose company we enjoy but who we're not really vulnerable with.

*Pastors need friends.* Or we have followers in the congregation who we can't be vulnerable with because it's counterproductive to do so.

This is why it is critical to have real friends, not just buddies and followers. The power of having someone you can call and spill your guts to cannot be overestimated. We all need that encouraging friend at times. Some of the best I've found are friends from previous ministry circles that I've moved away from. We all understand each other's pressures and we also know one another's hearts on a deep level.

**Rest.** Because of the spiritual and emotional pressures involved, you need established times of rest in your life. This includes something like the standard Monday Sabbath day off, but also times of retreat and fellowship with other pastors, and vacations with your family. You'll have to make yourself schedule them beforehand or else when the time comes, you'll be too busy; things will arise that will make you want to cancel them. But rest is important. You're not just carrying the weight of one life, but in some measure, the lives of your entire congregation.

I meet too many pastors who have at least one major area of out whack. They have stress, family problems, purity problems, or spiritual problems—and no-one to talk to about them. Or these issues arise within their nuclear family, which is just as important to deal with. If your wife is struggling, you need to make major adjustments right away to focus on her health—not next year or after you're done traveling, or eventually it will blow up in your face. I have been part of an otherwise strong church where the pastor's wife suffered a sudden mental breakdown. I have observed that many women will suffer silently, serving their ministry-minded husbands because they love them and want to please the Lord. Yet one day you wake up to an unpleasant surprise.

Similarly, if your devotional life is weak, then you should band together with some other pastors and ministry leaders to be a part of a group that will feed your own faith and walk. If you don't have friends that you can be open, honest and comfortable with, then it is like planning to have a meltdown.

I'm not saying that you are going to live in 10/10 perfection in all of these areas. That unrealistic standard will only become its own cause of failure. But you should take an honest inventory of the core areas and make sure your foundations in each of these areas are secure before you start trying to build bigger—or your house is likely to fall as soon as real weight comes on it. The biggest issues that can sink a pastor are summed by the famous saying: "The Girls, The Gold, and the Glory."

## THE GIRLS: MAINTAINING PURITY

Perhaps one of the most difficult topics in church life, and especially contemporary church life, is maintaining a culture of purity. In the wake of sexual revolution of the 1960's, we have lost the cultural supports which helped keep relationships pure and wholesome. We have entered into a brave new world where anything goes, and that's hard to keep out of church.

As you certainly already know, if you as the pastor have a moral failure, it will crash your church and your ministry. But there is a subsidiary issue – that even if you yourself are morally pure, but you have a major moral issue with leadership in your church, it's still a disaster. It's important to realize how much the cues you send to the congregation create the atmosphere for everyone else. There's protective and life-giving covering if purity flows down from the top.

Some churches deal with this subject by building strict rules around gender relations, but this usually leads to legalism. How can you create a healthy atmosphere without that? The best way to deal with the situation is to create a culture of heartfelt purity on your leadership team, starting with yourself. This culture will radiate outwards from the center and affect the whole body without deteriorating into a list of do's and don'ts.

Talk with your core team about it on occasion. Solicit input and troubleshoot questions that make sense for your local context. Make sure that they have transparent relationships with others that make them more resistant to temptation. This means close friends, usually not on the team, who are mature and stable who will support their purity as well as other aspects of being a success.

If you are a man getting into church leadership for the first time, you will probably be surprised by the amount of temptation you face. Your position as the leader of a congregation, and as a stable and spiritual man, makes you the center of attention and very attractive to women, and statistically speaking there are more women at church than men. But temptation goes both ways, female leaders get a lot of attention and affirmation from men which can cause temptation, and they are also in contact with far more high quality men than in any other normal situation. ("The Guys, the Gold and the Glory").

This is why everyone needs healthy boundaries. I'm not going to go into extensive details, but the key thing you need to avoid as the pastor is private personal interactions with people of the opposite sex, most especially those where there is the potential for attraction in either direction. In our electronic era, it is probably even more important to hold to this pattern in the virtual world where no one is watching at all.

Our senior leadership does a remarkably good job at this.

They keep a very strong relationship with their spouse, with interactions with members of the opposite sex on the professional side, and avoid the kinds of private or personal interactions that could lead to trouble. They do a lot of things together! And they copy each other on electronic communications.

I also personally work to avoid creating the kind of private space that could lead to temptation, especially on the phone or online. I include my wife or other people on text threads so that even a personal message is not a private message. I am always looking to include my wife in my ministry activities in ways that fit her personality. We pray together as altar workers and in prayer meetings. We try to minister together or bring one another into each other's spaces and audiences. It's not a a legalistic thing. The goal is simply for you and your spouse to be visible in your physical and virtual spheres, and to be generally seen as a couple by others...and by yourself! Then there is covering and no space for the enemy to work with.

## THE GOLD

Pastors face a structural temptation when it comes to dealing with money. Outside the church, most careers are salary or wage-based – you are paid a certain amount based on an agreement with an employer. Your pay can increase slightly if you do well for your employer, but you do not have any direct control over that. Since you don't control the main source of potential income, there is very little temptation.

However, in some careers that are sales-based, there is the potential for increase based or your ability to recruit or sell to others. In these careers, there is potential to increase your wealth based on how you treat others, which can lead not just to temptation, but to structural pressure to exploit others for wealth. This is where we get the image of the "used car salesman." The nature of his work incentivizes him to be less than honest.

In a few elite careers, you can make money simply based

on your celebrity or talent. You can experience exponential income growth overnight by your followers increasing. In these careers, the temptation is toward vanity, since people are paying for you to be you.

Structurally speaking, pastors face both of these kinds of temptation. Most also have the additional power that few in any kind of business have – the ability to change the rules. More than that, you set the culture surrounding gain and giving. By the way you preach and teach, you can either create an environment of joyful giving, or one of exploitation. As leader and interpreter of the Word of God, you have great power to affect not only how much people give, but their rationale and beliefs behind it.

This is especially if you are not in a denominational context where there are pre-existing checks and balances to keep you safe. Make sure that whatever system you are in, has checks and balances. These aren't just to protect others from you, they are to protect you from you. Remember, absolute power corrupts absolutely.

When you have a small congregation, the temptations are usually invisible, as you are experiencing the challenges that come from having little. But when pastors achieve success, your character is then tested in the same way that both the salesman's and the celebrity's are.

I once visited the church of a famous pastor who had been known for his powerful role in the days of revival. He was raising money for some kind of campaign and had a giant silver chalice placed in the middle of the church. During the service, he preached about how he was never going to become one of those pastors who was focused on money, but then encouraged everyone to give into the silver chalice! I believe he was blinded by his belief in the nobility of his cause from seeing the culture it created around him.

Others are less noble. They realize that if they preach in the right way, the offering will increase and so will their salary.

The church then migrates from being a path to salvation to a path of remuneration. When you start thinking and preaching about money too much, you may be starting down the slippery slope. There is no shame in cutting your budget if you need to in order to keep the pressure off of you. If you grow God's people, over time He will grow the budget.

The variations of how money can be abused are almost endless. Another pastor I know, when funds became short, used predesignated funds to pay his salary, while at the same time paying others next to nothing. This crushed the hearts of those who worked for him and who sacrificed for the fund. As a pastor, you have great spiritual authority over your flock and therefore also have a great duty not to put undue pressure on them to give. You must steward the resources they entrust to you wisely before the Lord, but also their hearts. We want people to give freely with pure motives. When the pressure goes up, an invisible price starts being paid as they give without the grace to do so.

Aim to be above reproach in this area and entrust faithful elders with like-minded hearts around your finances as well. When Billy Graham started in ministry, many considered evangelists to be unethical people who raised money off the gospel, so he made the resolution that he would have a real Board with the authority to set his pay, and that his pay would be set to match that of a pastor in a typical large city. This shielded him from the temptations that exponential wealth from becoming the world's most famous evangelist could have caused him. In the process, it also restored the good name of evangelists. He became the gold-standard for not loving Gold and ushered in a new era of trust toward the ministry – and his family and ministry were exceedingly blessed in the process.

Having a real Board around you that sets your pay and reviews the salaries of your team is an important step of accountability and part of best business practices. In addition, your salaried positions should be keyed using publicly available information. Our church follows the standard policy of capping both salary and facility expenses to a certain percentage of our overall income, which prevents several layers of temptation.

## THE GLORY

Fame does funny things to people, even if you are only famous to the people you know! If you obtain any measure of success and status, you may discover something about yourself that you do not like. You'll have to grow in the Lord through the process so that it doesn't sink your career just as it gets going.

As Lord Acton put it, "Power corrupts, and absolute power corrupts absolutely." A successful pastor can develop a kind of absolute power since they control people's view of God. In addition, pastors *are* a kind of local celebrity. We get up on stage every week and all of the most important people in our lives listen to all the important counsel we have to give them for half an hour. We're a role model and guide.

This leads to the temptations that come with celebrity status. We easily become beholden to what others think about us. We love the praise, and sink on the disappointments. We are thrilled when a new family joins, and heartbroken when one leaves. If we're honest with ourselves, many of us are a bit awed by the ultra-successful pastors in our stream, and treat them with their own kind of celebrity. It's not something we do intentionally; it's part of the structure that we have to proactively resist or it grows on its own.

While these mindsets are normal and part of the growth process as a leader, if we feed them, they can cross us over into dangerous vanity. If you feed the culture of celebrity around you it will grow. You find yourself acting and thinking in ways that make you seem better than the others in the church. My pastor does things like having people call him by his first name, rather than "Pastor," especially by the core team, for this reason. Although he is more famous than many pastors, and has had a lot of success, he's down to earth because he's chosen not to feed it.

Perhaps the greatest glory we can experience, however, is when the Spirit of God is moving through us. It's an intoxicating high that some anointed ministers have said is more powerful than any drug. The high of having people transformed through your prayer, your words, or your touch is incredible...and so is the letdown. This can lead to becoming a kind of "ministry addict," where the high of ministry replaces the love of Jesus. This will make your power or gifting becomes the rudder of your life. Anyone familiar with church history and movements knows this has destroyed many leaders and many churches.

Ironically, the opposition that comes with having an anointed ministry is often sufficient to prevent our ego from inflating too much! I believe that is what Paul's thorn in 2 Corinthians 12:7 was about. On a daily basis, I think the key is that we stay rooted in love. When love dominates our motives, ego does not have a lot of room. This goes back to the importance of family, devotional, and rest that we mentioned earlier. These keep us rooted and grounded.

Secondly, we have to resist building up the idea that because of the anointing, we are "the man of God" when we enter the room. I have been part of several churches with this kind of culture. They had their leadership bring them water, carry their bags, etc. You were awed if one of them chose you to drive them to the airport or babysit their children. The end result of this kind of culture is always bad because it teaches us to honor men over God.

While it is important that your congregation have a healthy culture of respect for leadership, it should be mostly invisible. Even if some people do think you are a celebrity, it's important to be just a regular guy to those closest to you, especially your family. By making yourself vulnerable in this way, you keep yourself humble. Jesus, of course, is the greatest possible role model of this, having humbled Himself to take on the form of a man (Phil 2:8). Part of the power of Jesus' humility was in being a regular guy – the kind of guy who went to weddings and dinner parties, and served others by washing their feet and feeding them.

## LIVING IN TORNADO ALLEY

The last bullet coming at pastors is church conflict. Some are worse than others, but every senior leader faces them. I call these special kinds of conflicts that emerge in the church "tornados." They get stirred up between two people over something that might not seem big at first, but if we're not careful they can grow and begin to siphon everyone else into them, destroying everything in its path.

In my former career in I/T, I was insulated from most tornadoes by the fact that everyone was paid to work, and they were fired if they did not. The church, however, is a volunteer organization where people come to express their passion. This means they are highly invested in how things are, and yet, have no natural guardrails on their behavior beyond social norms. This makes the church the perfect breeding ground for tornados.

Probably the most common issue that Christian leaders face is backbiting or gossip. Christians tend to be much more conflict averse then non-believers because we value leadership and care about how others feel. This leads us to vent our frustrations with each other instead of addressing the source of the problem with the appropriate leaders. In a church, this behavior can easily escalate into a tornado, especially if you respond by gossiping back or jumping into the mud with the offending party. Avoid the temptation of building your own band of friends to defend you, or of preaching a Sunday sermon against gossip when you suddenly discover you are under attack. This brings you down to the level of the person you are struggling with.

The first, best thing to do in conflict is to treat the

offending party exceptionally well. Give them no excuse to malign you further. Sometimes a person's small offense will go away after they have had time to reflect on it, just because it is not given more fuel. Or someone else who knows your character may come along and diffuse their bomb for you.

When that's not enough, the best thing to do is exactly what they failed to do: approach them directly. Remember you have a lot of invisible power as the leader, even if you aren't feeling it at the moment. Avoid the temptation to use your power and authority to intimidate them. Try to create an environment that is relational and invite them to share their concerns with you directly. Then ask them if they can do that in the future. You might walk out with an ally instead of an enemy. When we go in with guns blazing, the end result is to energize the conflict.

*Positive culture detoxifies a church.* Just as negativity is a powerful destroyer, positivity is a powerful shaper. Positive culture detoxifies a church. By being positive and deemphasizing divisive doctrines, you can take a lot of ammunition away from those who love to start controversy. I've found that many people prone to conflict will often simply get tired of not having something to seize on, get frustrated, and move on.

It's critical to avoid inserting negative energy into the equation whenever possible. The enemy's goal with a tornado is to get you to insert negativity into the culture of your church. Accusations and dissent break out when people see the pastor or his staff get frustrated and get in the flesh — even if it was completely warranted. In essence, in a church conflict, the person who goes negative loses. As you practice staying positive, you stay on the top side of conflicts. On the other hand, when you go negative, that negative energy gets released into the system of your church and will express itself somewhere. Don't take the bait and put the negativity into the system yourself!

I believe that rising above any negative behaviors of your congregation and any false accusations that come at you is one of the most difficult and important tests of pastoral leadership. Jesus spells it out this way:

> If you love only those who love you, why should you get credit for that? Even sinners love those who love them! (Matt. 5:46)

If we just are good to our supporters, that's a low level of leadership common in the world. But when we are able to rise above, we are modeling the personality of Jesus. We're sowing into that supernatural realm of love which the Lord honors. People try to bring down, but the Lord promotes (Luke 14:10-11).

Having been through my own share of accusations and dust-ups, I have come to understand that a key part of success lies in being able to believe better for a person than their behavior is currently showing. When we allow ourselves to define a person by their behavior, we are agreeing with the enemy's plans for their life. Instead, we must choose to believe and hope for better, even if the person forces us to close doors of opportunity for them.

None of this means that you let destructive behavior run wild in the church. I will say more about that in a minute. It just means that by principle, you do not energize conflicts, you confront only when needed, and you believe the best for and about the person who is causing the issue.

Besides tornadoes you're in the center of, there are those that start in your midst. Sometimes two people with noticeable character flaws get into a skirmish and then begin drawing as many people as possible into it. The best way to deal with any tornado is to drain its energy away. Your jumping in the middle will tend to feed its energy and drag even more people in, while putting your pastoral prestige on the line which is an important part of what holds the church together. Don't allow someone's personal conflict to become a church conflict by jumping in the middle. If someone has not followed Matthew 18 by going to their brother first, don't take it up as the pastor, and definitely never take sides.

For example, when dealing with a serious marital conflict, it's better to involve a professional counselor. They are trained to deal with these things, and if they give advice that the couple rejects, it reflects on them, not on the entire church. When dealing with conflict among your members, professional distance is your friend. Remember, anytime you are perceived as being in a conflict, your pastoral prestige is at risk. You only want to use the power of your office when you have to in order to maintain a healthy body.

Importantly, you and your spouse should agree on how much you discuss church matters. Your spouse should be your number one support and you need them in order to survive, but they can get into conflicts by proxy and take the conflict even harder than you because they are rooting for you. Your spouse needs to practice the same kind of professional distance from conflicts that you do. If either one of you gets into a deep partisan conflict, it hurts you both.

Of course, not every church member is a positive and productive member. There are always those people whom you want to lead out the back door. These are people who cause trouble and are not willing to address their own behaviors. We want to honor the Lord by giving these people real chances to repent and grow, but we also want to protect the sheep by helping them to move on when they resist.

Helping these people to exit gracefully is one of the arts of a great pastor. The memorable story of one of America's most famous pastors goes that when he reached the end of the line with a particular person, he put his arm around him and said simply, "John, I'm resigning as your pastor today." Both of them understood that the pastor was not going anywhere, but was artfully asking this difficult man to leave.

Prayer is an important part of all of this. A friend of mine was in a rough dust-up involving four different families in the church who falsely accused and maligned him. He knew he was in the right, and that their actions would have spiritual consequences. He watched over the following year as they each went into family turmoil. A prophet came to him, however, and said "God isn't happy with how you treated your brothers." He was dumbfounded until the prophet said, "You were supposed to pray for them." God doesn't want the worst for our enemies, and just as importantly, he wants us to be models of his kindness and patience toward those who make themselves enemies.

On your own staff, there will always be some level of conflict whether you can see it or not. As the leader, these are the ones you should proactively work on. Some of this is preventative. Having fun and relational times together as a team is like putting oil into the engine—it reduces the friction so that work can be done.

In addition, it's good to coach your team on healthy conflict resolution before one arises. Encourage your team to use Matthew 18 on each other. I've found that most of the time this will eliminate conflict and gossip between well-meaning people. When tension is building, they should lean in relationally and try to work it out. If that fails, you need to involve yourself to help them smooth it over and resolve it. If you sense one or both parties need coaching, it's better to do that privately.

These are just a few of the most common church conflict scenarios. It's a standard job hazard. Yet if you stay positive, don't feed tornadoes with energy, and confront when necessary, you can avoid many conflicts and keep your flock on mission.

# Putting the Pieces Together

## TROUBLESHOOTING YOUR CHURCH

Hopefully by this point you understand what an encounter-based church is and how it differs from prevailing models. By making encounter with Jesus the priority, and building systems within your church to facilitate encounters and follow up on the results, you can both gather a large number of people and see deep and authentic change. I've given you a lot of tactics and insights that flow from this perspective, but the question you may be asking now is: how do I put it all together?

Let's go back to the ministry funnel presented in the Systems chapter:

A healthy church has a large funnel of people flowing into it, a strong core in the middle, and a another large funnel of committed people who are doing the work. If your church has that, then there is a good chance you are growing well already and are probably do not need this book. The three models below, however, lay out why there can be challenges in this area.

The most common is the "community church." The community church does not have a strong outreach system or a strong ministry system. It is comprised of people who have known each other for a long time and love to be together, probably live near each other, and do the things they have always done. Churches in this model often have congregations in the low hundreds. The risk is that the church will stagnate and die out over time if steps are not taken to adjust it. The funnel looks something like this:

Community Church

The key thing in the community church is to break up the inward focus by building the other two ends of the funnel: Outreach and Leadership. And the activities in the Growth and Ministry activities should restructured to have goals. Any change you make will likely cause some friction, but if you are wise in the steps you are taking then this friction is actually a sign that you are breaking the old, inwardly focused model.

The second most common broken pattern is the "ministry church." The ministry church is usually comprised of very mature and very committed Christians who are serving hard, going after God, and doing life together. This is the most common model for vibrant churches or house churches with 75 or fewer people. Its funnel looks like the diagram below. A lot of powerful ministry is going on, but the church isn't growing because there is no Outreach system. Often the Leadership system is weak as well.

Ministry Church

The way out of this box is to "re-launch" by holding events and creating the attractional components in the same way you would with a new church plant – build up to a launch event over a period of several months, with a big marketing push and show your ministry-oriented team how this is going to lead to a much broader ministry opportunity.

The last model is the "outreach church." This one can be misleading because it might not look completely fine to the leadership. This church could be 500 or even 1000 people but it's not growing the way it could be. Discipleship and going deeper with God is lacking.

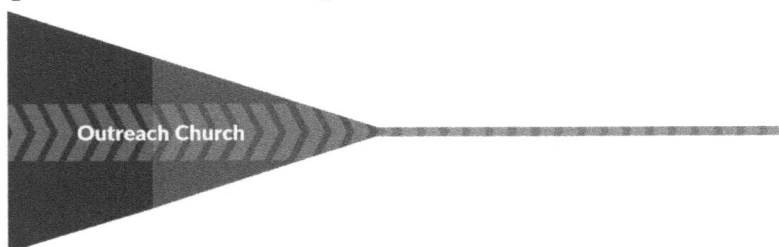

You know you are leading an outreach church if you regularly see new faces, but your overall numbers aren't going up much. This means that the outreach systems are working to pull people in, but the Ministry and Leadership systems are weak or broken, so that people are just not sticking.

There are lots of potential pieces that could be missing here, but the most likely is that you need to restructure around encounter. To fix this church, you will have to shift some of your energy downstream to the more relational and spiritual components. You've perfected the systems which bring people, but you need to build the systems which change and retain them. In addition to retuning the service toward encounter, take a look a things like the growth pipeline for leaders, the ability to connect from Sunday to ministry opportunities.

## ASSEMBLING THE COMPONENTS

On the next page, you will find a diagram of all of the major components of the encounter-based church. It's probably too ambitious to build them all at once, but seeing them together can help you to tune and identify things you can do now. Below I have outlined the logical steps of priority to get from where you are, to where you want to go.

**1. Create the Encounter.** The first and most important part is to tune your Sunday experience to focus on encounter. If you have already built an excellent service from an attractional paradigm, this probably means opening up room intentionally for the Holy Spirit in some of the ways mentioned. If you have a traditional service, it probably means moving away from some traditions in order to get more focus on the Holy Spirit and also how things look. Along with this, you should begin to organize your people so that you have real service teams supporting the service, and make sure that those teams are functioning from a paradigm that sees you as the leader and really places priority on vertical and horizontal encounter.

You're not going to get anywhere without prayer, so you should at least have prayed together with your leaders. Or you could build a broader prayer meeting around your more passionate people. It's a logical next step to feed encounter, building off the Sunday service where you engage the church in believing God will do mighty things.

**2. Build the Off-Ramps from Service.** Once your Sunday service is tuned, you need to make sure it leads somewhere. If you were to build Outreach first, you'd have new fish jumping in the boat before you had anywhere to put them. This is why you have to get your nets ready.

This means that Next Steps and Growth Groups should be built, as well as the communication systems to support them and leaders to run them. You'll need tools like "connection cards" to capture the information of guests and a ready list of opportunities to serve that fit a variety of different maturity levels in God for people to start taking the journey.

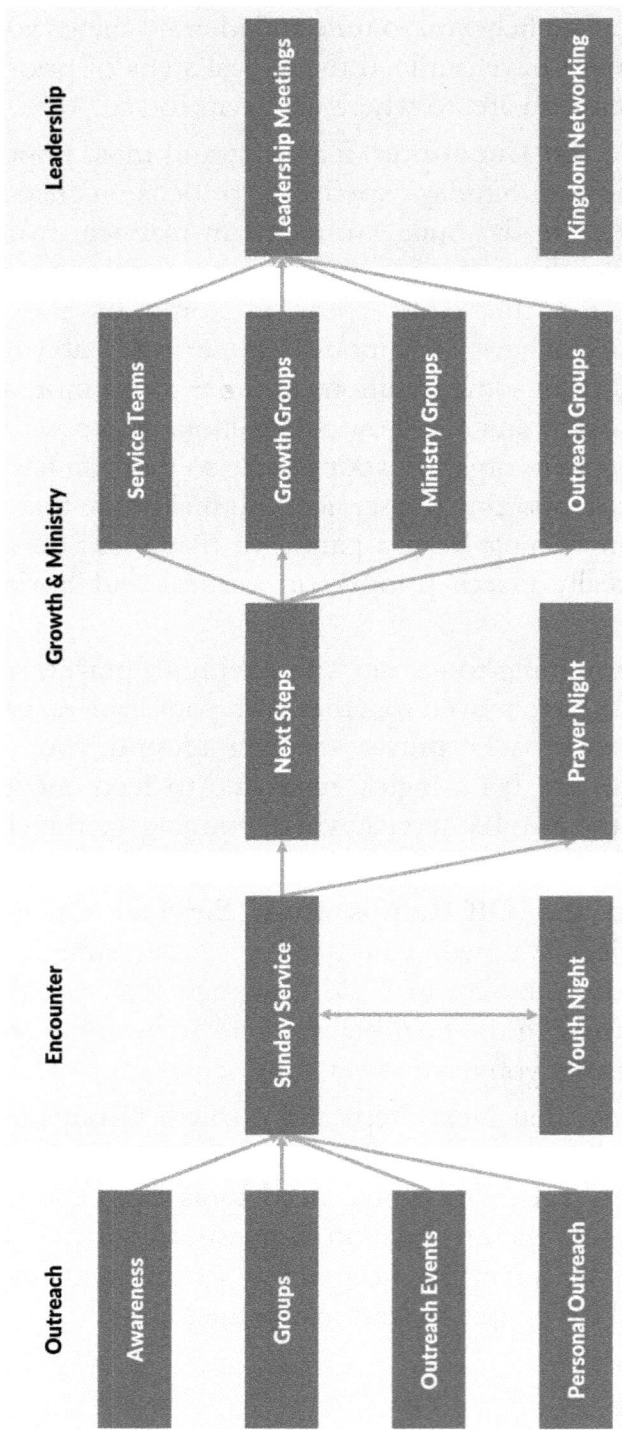

**3. Build the On-Ramps.** Now that you have the basic plumbing in place, you can begin to add the Outreach and Awareness System which is going to draw people to your church to check it out. Examine all of the outward-facing activities and communications, including email or sign-up newsletters, service projects, etc., and start to engage your church in the process. As the awareness function gets going, you can leverage it to start hosting certain days and events intentionally designed to connect with people.

**4. Build Supporting Systems.** From this point you can add other components as you are able. Ministry Groups are essential for retention and referral, so begin to identify leaders and initiate groups or classes where you have grace to do so. Now is also a good time to bring the Youth Group into alignment with the encounter-based model. This may involve a relaunch event to get fresh momentum.

**5. Enhancement.** Once these key systems of the church in place, you can enhance it. Outreach groups can be added and expanded as you have capacity and grace. You yourself can also start to look outward to weddings, city-wide prayer meetings, or other activities that give you more face time with your local community. The Kingdom-oriented components discussed in the Leadership and Growth systems can also be added at this point.

Of course, the nature of your situation and capacity will vary quite widely, but by taking growth and change in logical phases, you can make a lot of distance without destroying what already exists.

BUILDING YOUR TEAM

I would speculate that every pastor has a set of "fantasy hires" if they had the budget to do it. But then, if you had the budget, you would have already done it! So we have to build our teams with volunteer support and the resources we have.

On the next page I have a suggested organizational chart

to run an encounter-based church. The darker shade is for the most important roles, which would most likely require a full-time paid staff member. The lighter shade is for roles that can emerge as your church grows. Of course every church is different, and every situation is different, so this is only a proposal, but I hope it will help you to think through who is on your team and what roles they can play.

One of the most important things to notice is that you as the Senior Pastor need two pastoral people supporting you who have different gift mixes. On the one side of the chart you have an Executive Pastor underneath you. This is someone who knows how to make the trains run. Without them, everything is harder and things get missed. They may have a professional background in project management or another highly operational job, or they may be someone who has come up through your Leadership system. All the complex operational functions of the church report to the Executive Pastor. The Executive Pastor is, by extension, the person most responsible for the components that make the Sunday service and related events happen.

On the other side is an Associate Pastor underneath you. This is someone who is very relationally wired. Their orientation toward people and relationships is essential for the ministry functions they oversee to function well. The Associate leads the ministry oriented teams and is the focal point in the church for ensuring that people find the right places to receive ministry. They take some of the personal pressures off of the Executive so that they can concentrate on leading and speaking. The Associate is critical relationally on Sundays but the pieces they oversee happen mostly outside of service.

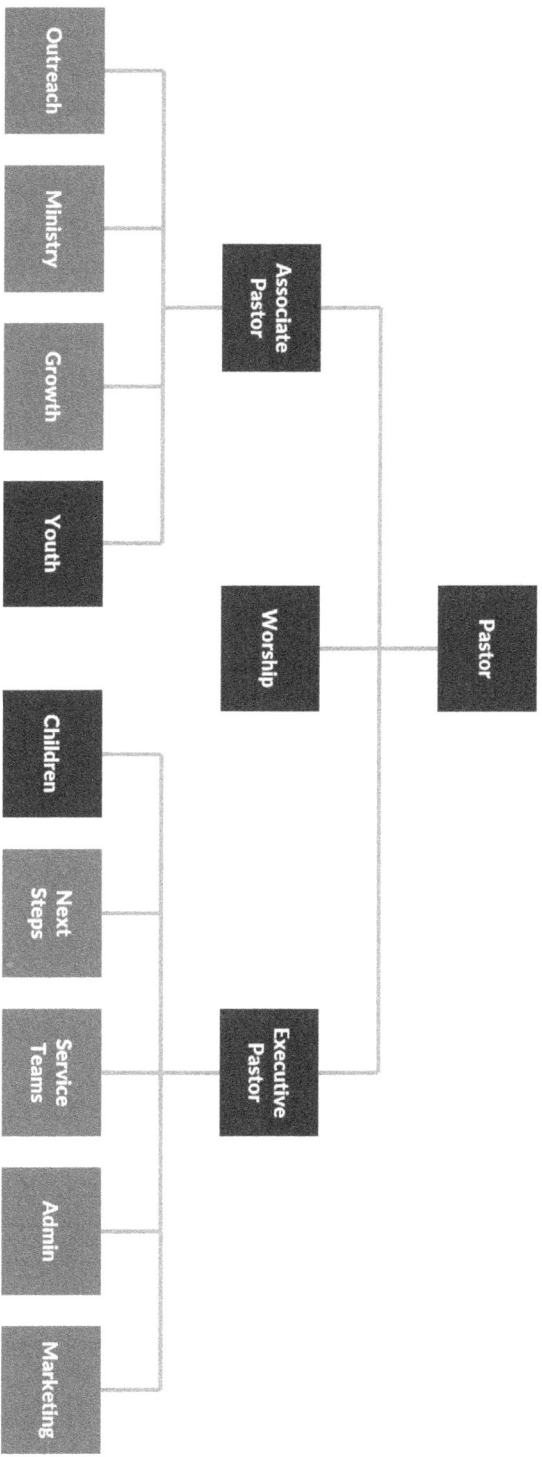

```
Pastor
├── Associate Pastor
│   ├── Outreach
│   ├── Ministry
│   ├── Growth
│   └── Youth
├── Worship
└── Executive Pastor
    ├── Children
    ├── Next Steps
    ├── Service Teams
    ├── Admin
    └── Marketing
```

You can see on the diagram that there are two separate reporting chains, one to the Executive and one to the Associate Pastor. These two separate reporting chains provide you with a great separation of duties, allowing for specialization, and preventing your church from tilting out of balance. This is also why it important that both report directly to you as the Senior Leader. You will be shifted in the direction of what you hear all the time. It's easy to become too operationally focused, or not sufficiently operationally focused, and then balls get dropped.

Looking at the diagram, you'll see the ministry oriented pieces, which mostly take place outside of Sundays are under the Associate, while the operationally oriented pieces which mostly take place on Sundays are under the Executive. It might seem strange to separate Children and Youth but they are pictured this way because Children's ministry is often primarily an operational challenge on Sundays, while Youth Ministry is like an entire church running during the rest of the week.

It's important to note though, that both of these roles have to have some capability in the other side. If you have someone who is everybody's best friend but can't get through his inbox as the Associate, then he won't be able to run the functions underneath him. Conversely, if you have someone who so operational that they struggle with personal connections, then they will have a hard time leading their teams.

Most professional organizations have a similar split. At Prison Fellowship, we have a COO who runs all the administrative functions, and then we have several ministry Vice Presidents who are experts in their part of the ministry. Many public companies have Senior Executives responsible for their lines of business, and then have other key personnel such as HR and Legal also reporting directly to the CEO. This is because it's essential that each of those voices is heard in the CEO's office for him or her to run a successful enterprise.

Also at the top of your chart is your worship leader. The

worship function is so central to an encounter-based church that they are usually one of your first hires, even if it is not a full-time position. You need someone who is called to worship, is humble, and brings in the presence of God—and who can build a team around them. This is a high bar. Depending on their capacity they could also lead other parts of the church. Since their role involves a lot of production but is also relational in nature, having them report directly to you can help keep organizational balance.

None of this means that this is the only way to structure your teams. There are many ways that may make sense based on the particular skills and maturity of the people involved as well as the exact nature and scope of the ministries. Pastors have heavy speaking and organizational responsibilities which can cause them to want to outsource the entire organization to a single COO figure, but the risk this always creates is that you become distant from your staff and what is happening in the church. This is why I advocate for several direct reports holding major portions of the church responsibility.

## WHO ARE THE STAFF?

Beneath each of the core roles, in the lighter shades, are roles that oversee each of the other systems. In the beginning, these roles are owned by the Executive and Associate, but as you grow they can become lead volunteers, and eventually paid staff.

As anyone who has ever done it knows, staffing a church is a very complicated proposition. How do you know who to pay and how much to pay them? People who are seasoned and highly competent are also often under other financial and time pressures which means that hiring them is going to be expensive. Someone who is college-age will be more affordable and simpler to lead. People are almost always willing to work for less money to do more ministry because of the intangible benefit of being able to be paid to make a difference. Should you build a lot of inexpensive staff, or do you bring in seasoned people?

In terms of who you pay, the simple answer is: pay more for the people who make the biggest impact on the organization. Your full- time staff should be people who, by hiring them, increases your effectiveness exponentially.

The second consideration should be to look at roles which are hardest to do and replace. There are any number of ways you can slice these roles. Because of how essential children's ministry and worship are to the success of your church, for example, these are also potential considerations to hire. But so much of these jobs is geared towards Sunday that you may be able to get away with a part time role while you are small.

Some roles may be able to be performed by someone on a stipend rather than full-time staff. With this mindset, hiring key volunteer leaders as part-time employees can be a win for all, as long as you keep the expectations narrow enough to allow the rest of their life to work. This gives them an incentive to do the job well, and it gives you more leverage in directing them.

## TRACKING YOUR PROGRESS

*Anything that can be measured (within reason) should be measured.*

Measuring your progress is essential to being successful at anything. As I have been coaching pastors to employ these s ystems, I have come to believe that anything that can be measured (within reason) should be measured. Good data tells you stories, stories that you need to grow.

My initial role at Prison Fellowship was Director of Operations, and my job was to put systems in place and measurements that would lead us back to growth. Before we had these metrics and started accurately tracking, we had a wildly incorrect view of how much we were actually accomplishing. Developing metrics allowed us to identify not only how much we were doing, but who the right staff were and whether or not we were really being successful. Measuring results is part of telling ourselves the truth, and creating a cycle of continuous improvement.

The most basic metric of your church that every pastor knows is your **Sunday attendance**. Knowing it and tracking it are not exactly the same, however. When you start careful tracking of your Sunday attendance you will start to notice patterns like peaks around Christmas and Easter, and dips during the summer. When you compare these year over year, you will be able to identify if you are really growing or not and also you will have information about how to leverage momentum. In, fact every metric we discuss here should be looked at from a year/year basis because of the seasonal nature of church participation. This is even more true if you live in the far north or other extreme climate.

The limitation of Sunday attendance is that it's the downstream result of so much other activity. It's a little bit like looking at the corporate bottom line – you know whether or not you are making money, but without more information you don't know why and whether or not it will continue. Other things that are easy to count may also not be particularly informative because they measure activity, rather than results.

In crime statistics, for example, this is the reason why murder rate is so important. The amount of policing you are doing can have a huge impact on how many drug busts you have, and therefore create an illusion of either more or less crime going on, but you can't fake the murder rate. Comparing the number of murders between cities gives a much better perspective of how dangerous a city really is – for every one murder we can assume that many other crimes occur regardless of whether or not they were caught.

What this means is that counting your raw number of small groups, for example, as not as informative as one might hope because it is a measure of how much is going on, not how *effective* that activity is at producing the intended results. Baptisms is also a common and easily tracked number, but for this to be really valuable information you should separate child baptisms, re-baptisms, and baptisms as a result of adult conversion because each tells you something quite different. While I still believe you should count and track trends of any key activity you are doing, *be careful about what these numbers are actually telling you.* For example, the number of baptisms your church sees may be simply a result of how much or little you are emphasizing baptism.

Counting **connection cards** is a very good metric because it can show the result of your outreach activity. The number of new people coming in the door is a result of either people finding you on the internet, being touched by an outreach activity, or being referred by a friend. In a small to medium sized church, I think the extra effort of really identifying where people are coming in from is some of the most valuable leg-work you can possibly do. You want to know: Are people coming in because they saw your sign? Because a friend invited them? Because they joined a group? Identifying where people are coming from tells you what to do more of, and can also help you spotlight pockets of life in your congregation.

If you track your total number of connection cards in a month and compare that to your total attendance change for the month, you can get an approximation of your **retention rate.** If your average attendance went up by 25 during the month, and you had 50 cards, that would be a (very high) retention rate of 50% for guests. Of course this obscures the a lot of things like people leaving your church, seasonal factors, and those who prefer not to fill out the cards, but tracking it will still tell you a lot. Make sure to ask if people are first time visitors, returning visitors, or just looking for ministry, to help make that accurate.

Your **Next Steps attendance** is an essential metric as well. Assuming you are also marketing that well, this number tells you how many people are going from attending the Sunday service to wanting to be more deeply involved in your church. When you look at this in conjunction with your visitor cards, you can get a sense of your "conversion rate" – what percentage of new people make it past the front door into the back office.

**Adult Conversions** may be the most valuable metric of all, but it is not as easy to obtain as one would think. These are people that did not go to church and did not have a relationship with Jesus before they came to your church. Usually a person who has truly converted creates significant waves in the life of a church so you can tell. You can often get this number by a hand count in discussion with your leadership team each month. On this point, don't be afraid to apply the definition of "conversion" narrowly – remember for every one adult conversion, there is a great deal of other ministry going on that is also valuable. You can supplement this number by looking at attendance of Foundations classes which are designed for new or rededicated believers.

In addition to ongoing measurements, surveys can be helpful to understanding where your congregation is. The **Net Promoter Score** discussed in the Ministry chapter is a great focal point for a survey to analyzing how likely your church is to grow – since a great deal of growth comes from referral, you have to build a culture where people are outward focused. By asking the question "How Likely are you to recommend our church to a friend?" And storing it you can discover how much positive energy and potential you have built up in the congregation. If the NPS is low, then it gives you an opportunity to work on different areas that may be preventing people from referring friends, including whether the right systems exist, whether people have unmet needs, and whether they are really equipped to reach to friends.

CONCLUSION

The encounter-based church model is ultimately about

obedience to the First and Second Commandment. If we love Jesus and lift Him up, we know that He will draw all men (John 12:32). We create spaces and opportunities for Him to encounter people. We don't have to face a dichotomy between welcoming Him and doing things that bring people. We set the table for the feast where He can come and dine, and we enjoy His presence. We also love others and value the gifts in each other, which is another way people encounter the true love of Christ.

This mindset is the core of the encounter-based paradigm. If we love each other well, and are great vehicles for Jesus to love others through us, then lives will be changed and the Kingdom will come on earth as it is in heaven.

www.ingramcontent.com/pod-product-compliance
Lightning Source LLC
Chambersburg PA
CBHW071957040426
42447CB00009B/1377